REVELATION

Chapters 1—5

J. Vernon McGee

THOMAS NELSON
Since 1798

NASHVILLE   DALLAS   MEXICO CITY   RIO DE JANEIRO

Published in Nashville, Tennessee, by Thomas Nelson, Inc.

Scripture quotations are from the KING JAMES VERSION of the Bible.

Library of Congress Cataloging-in-Publication Data

McGee, J. Vernon (John Vernon), 1904–1988
  [Thru the Bible with J. Vernon McGee]
  Thru the Bible commentary series / J. Vernon McGee.
    p.   cm.
  Reprint. Originally published: Thru the Bible with J. Vernon
McGee. 1975
  Includes bibliographical references.
  ISBN 0-7852-1064-4 (TR)
  ISBN 0-7852-1121-7 (NRM)
  1. Bible—Commentaries. I. Title.
BS491.2.M37 1991
220.7'7—dc20   90-41340
ISBN: 978-0-7852-0895-2   CIP

Printed in the United States of America

41 42 QG 14 13

CONTENTS

REVELATION—Chapters 1—5

PREFACE

The radio broadcasts of the Thru the Bible Radio five-year program were transcribed, edited, and published first in single-volume paperbacks to accommodate the radio audience.

There has been a minimal amount of further editing for this publication. Therefore, these messages are not the word-for-word recording of the taped messages which went out over the air. The changes were necessary to accommodate a reading audience rather than a listening audience.

These are popular messages, prepared originally for a radio audience. They should not be considered a commentary on the entire Bible in any sense of that term. These messages are devoid of any attempt to present a theological or technical commentary on the Bible. Behind these messages is a great deal of research and study in order to interpret the Bible from a popular rather than from a scholarly (and too-often boring) viewpoint.

We have definitely and deliberately attempted "to put the cookies on the bottom shelf so that the kiddies could get them."

The fact that these messages have been translated into many languages for radio broadcasting and have been received with enthusiasm reveals the need for a simple teaching of the whole Bible for the masses of the world.

I am indebted to many people and to many sources for bringing this volume into existence. I should express my especial thanks to my secretary, Gertrude Cutler, who supervised the editorial work; to Dr. Elliott R. Cole, my associate, who handled all the detailed work with the publishers; and finally, to my wife Ruth for tenaciously encouraging me from the beginning to put my notes and messages into printed form.

Solomon wrote, ". . . of making many books there is no end; and much study is a weariness of the flesh" (Eccl. 12:12). On a sea of books that flood the marketplace, we launch this series of THRU THE BIBLE with the hope that it might draw many to the one Book, The Bible.

J. VERNON McGEE

REVELATION

INTRODUCTION

As we begin this Book of Revelation, I have mingled feelings. I am actually running scared as we come to this, one of the great books in the Word of God. Candidly, I must also say that it is with great joy that I begin it. Let me explain why I say this.

It has long been my practice, when I need a time of relaxation, to read a mystery story, a detective story. I confess that mystery stories have been more or less a hobby of mine over the years.

I do not read much of Agatha Christie anymore for the very simple reason that I have read so many of hers that I can usually figure out who the killer is, who committed the murder. Now I read Dorothy Sayers. By the way, she is a Christian, and she gets a great deal of Scripture into her books. The unsaved are reading the Bible without realizing it. Anyway, I have always enjoyed mystery stories.

When I began my ministry, I was a single man, and on Sunday nights after the evening service, I would get into bed and read one of the mystery stories.

Well, about one o'clock in the morning I would get to the place where the heroine has been tied down to the railroad tracks by the villain, and old Number 77 is going to be coming along in about twenty minutes. She is in a desperate situation. I think that the hero is going to be able to get there and rescue her, but I find out that he is in that old warehouse down by the pier, tied to a chair under which is a stick of dynamite with the fuse already lighted! Well, I can't leave the hero and heroine at one o'clock in the morning in that kind of position. But, since it is time for me to turn over and go to sleep, I slip over to the final page. A different scene greets me there. I see the hero and the heroine sitting out in a yard. I see a lovely cottage encircled by a white picket fence. They are married now and have a little baby who is playing there on the lawn. What a wonderful, comfortable scene that is!

So I would just turn back to the place where I stopped reading, and I would say to the hero and heroine, "I don't know how you are going to get out of it, but I tell you this: It's going to work out all right."

My friend, I have a book in the Bible called the Book of the Revelation, and it tells me how this world scene is going to end. I will be frank to say that I get a little disturbed today when I see what is happening in the world. It is a dark picture as I look out at it, and I wonder how it is going to work out. Well, all I do is turn to the last book of the Bible, and when I begin to read there, I find that it's going to work out all right. Do you know that? Emerson said that things are in the saddle, and they ride mankind. It does look that way. In fact, it looks as if the Devil is having a high holiday in the world, and I think he is, but God is going to work it out. God Himself will gain control—in fact, He has never lost control—and He is moving to the time when He is going to place His Son, the Lord Jesus Christ, upon the throne of His universe down here. It does look dark now. I think that any person today who looks at the world situation and takes an optimistic view of it has something wrong with his thinking. The world is in a desperate condition. However, I'm no pessimist because I have the Book of Revelation, and I can say to every person who has trusted Christ, "Don't you worry. It's going to work out all right." My friend, the thing is going to come out with God on top. Therefore, I want to be with Him. As Calvin put it, "I would rather lose now and win later than to win now and lose later." I want to say to you, friend, that I am on the side that appears to be losing now, but we are going to win later. The reason I know this is because I have been reading the Book of Revelation. And I hope that you are going to read it with me.

As I have said, I approach the Book of Revelation with fear and trembling, not primarily because of a lack of competence on my part (although that may be self-evident), but many other factors enter into this feeling. First of all, there may be a lack of knowledge on the part of the readers. You see, the Book of Revelation is the sixty-sixth brok of the Bible, and it comes last. This means that we need to know sixty-five other books before we get to this place. You need to have the background of a working knowledge of all the Bible that precedes it. You need to have a feel of the Scriptures as well as have the facts of the Scriptures in your mind.

There is a second factor that gives me a feeling of alarm as I enter this book. It is the contemporary climate into which we are giving these studies in Revelation. It is not primarily because of a skeptical and doubting age—although it is certainly that—but it is because of these dark and difficult and desperate days in which we live. We see the failure of leadership in every field—government, politics, science, education, military, and entertainment. Since the educators cannot control even their own campuses, how are they going to supply leadership for the world? Business is managed by tycoons. And the actors can be heard on the media talk programs. Listening to them for only a brief time reveals that they have nothing to say. They do a lot of talking, but they say nothing that is worthwhile. None of these groups or segments of our society have any solutions. They are failures in the realm of leadership. There is a glaring lack of leadership. There is no one to lead us out of this moral morass or out of the difficult and Laocoön-like problems which have us all tangled up. We are living in a very difficult time, my friend. In fact, I think that it is one of the worst in the history of the church.

Knowledgeable men have been saying some very interesting things about this present hour. Please note that I am not quoting from any preachers but from outstanding men in other walks of life.

Dr. Urey, from the University of Chicago, who worked on the atomic bomb, began an article several years ago in *Collier's* magazine by saying, "I am a frightened man, and I want to frighten you."

Dr. John R. Mott returned from a trip around the world and made the statement that this was "the most dangerous era the world has ever known." And he raised the question of where we are heading. Then he made this further statement, "When I think of human tragedy, as I saw it and felt it, of the Christian ideals sacrificed as they have been, the thought comes to me that *God is preparing the way for some immense direct action.*"

Chancellor Robert M. Hutchins, of the University of Chicago, gave many people a shock several years ago when he made the statement that "devoting our educational efforts to infants between six and twenty-one seems futile." And he added, "The world may not last long enough." He contended that for this reason we should begin adult education.

Winston Churchill said, "Time may be short."

Mr. Luce, the owner of *Life*, *Time*, and *Fortune* magazines, addressed a group of missionaries who were the first to return to their fields after the war. Speaking in San Francisco, he made the statement that when he was a boy, the son of a Presbyterian missionary in China, he and his father often discussed the premillennial coming of Christ, and he thought that all missionaries who believed in that teaching were inclined to be fanatical. And then Mr. Luce said, "I wonder if there wasn't something to that position after all."

It is very interesting to note that *The Christian Century* carried an article by Wesner Fallaw which said, "A function of the Christian is to make preparation for world's end."

Dr. Charles Beard, the American historian, said, "All over the world the thinkers and searchers who scan the horizon of the future are attempting to assess the values of civilization and speculating about its destiny."

Dr. William Yogt, in the *Road to Civilization*, wrote: "The handwriting on the wall of five continents now tells us that the Day of Judgment is at hand."

Dr. Raymond B. Fosdick, president of the Rockefeller Foundation, said, "To many ears comes the sound of the tramp of doom. Time is short."

H. G. Wells declared before he died, "This world is at the end of its tether. The end of everything we call life is close at hand."

General Douglas MacArthur said, "We have had our last chance."

Former president Dwight Eisenhower said, "Without a moral regeneration throughout the world there is no hope for us as we are going to disappear one day in the dust of an atomic explosion."

Dr. Nicholas Murray Butler, ex-president of Columbia University, said, "The end cannot be far distant."

To make the picture even more bleak, the modern church has no solutions for the problems of this hour in which we are living. There was a phenomenal growth in church membership, especially after World War II, but that took place for only a few years. The growth went from 20 percent of the population in 1884 to 35 percent of the population in 1959. That was the high point of Protestant church membership. And it would indicate the possibility of a church on fire for God. Then it had wealth and was building tremendous programs, but recently the church has begun to lose, and it certainly is not affecting the contemporary culture of the present hour.

As far back as 1958 the late David Lawrence wrote an editorial which he entitled "The 'Mess' in the World." He described it very accurately, but even he did not have a solution for it. As we look out at the world in this present hour, we see that it is really in a mess.

For a long time now men in high positions have looked into the future and have said that there is a great crisis coming. (I wonder what they would say if they lived in our day!) As a result of this foreboding, there has been a growing interest in the Book of Revelation.

Although good expositors differ on the details of the Book of Revelation, when it comes to the broad interpretation, there are four major systems. (Broadus lists seven theories of interpretation and Tregelles lists three.)

1. The preterist interpretation is that all of Revelation has been fulfilled in the past. It had to do with local references in John's day and with the days of either Nero or Domitian. This view was held by Renan and by most German scholars, also by Elliott. The purpose of the Book of Revelation was to bring comfort to the persecuted church and was written in symbols that the Christians of that period would understand.

Now let me say that it was for the comfort of God's people, and it has been that for all ages, but to hold the preterist interpretation means that you might as well take the Book of Revelation out of the Bible, as it has no meaning at all for the present hour. This viewpoint has been answered and, I think, relegated to the limbo of lost things.

2. The *historical* interpretation is that the fulfillment of Revelation is going on continuously in the history of the church, from John's day

to the present time. Well, I believe that there is a certain amount of truth in this as far as the seven churches are concerned, as we shall see, but beyond that, it is obvious that the Book of Revelation is prophetic.

3. The *historical-spiritualist* interpretation is a refinement of the historical theory and was advanced first by Sir William Ramsay. This theory states that the two beasts are imperial and provincial Rome and that the point of the book is to encourage Christians. According to this theory, Revelation has been largely fulfilled and contains only spiritual lessons for the church today.

The system we know today as amillennialism has, for the most part, adopted this view. It dissipates and defeats the purpose of the book. In the seminary of my denomination, I studied Revelation in both Greek and English from the standpoint of the amillennialist. It was amazing to see how the facts of the Revelation could be dissipated into thin air by just saying, "Well, these are symbols." But they never were able to tell us exactly what they were symbols of. That was their problem. The fact of the matter is that some very unusual interpretations arise from this viewpoint. One interpreter sees Luther and the Reformation in a symbol that to another student pictures the invention of the printing press! In my opinion, interpretations of this type have hurt and defeated the purpose of the Book of Revelation.

4. The *futurist* interpretation is the view which is held by all premillennialists and is the one which I accept and present to you. It sees the Book of Revelation as primarily prophetic. Most premillennialists follow a certain form of interpretation that conforms to the Book of Revelation. (We will see this in the outline of the book.) It begins with the revelation of the glorified Christ. Then the church is brought before us, and the whole history of the church is given. Then, at the end of chapter 3, the church goes to heaven and we see it, not as the church anymore, but as the bride which will come to the earth with Christ when He comes to establish His kingdom—that thousand-year reign that John will tell us about. It will be a time of testing, for at the end of that period Satan will be released for a brief season. Then the final rebellion is put down and eternity begins. This is the viewpoint of Revelation which is generally accepted.

In our day there are many critics of this interpretation who not only attempt to discount it but say rather harsh things about it. One recent book of criticism, written by a layman, quotes me as being unable to answer his argument. Well, the fact of the matter is that he called me at home one morning as I was getting ready to go to my office. I wasn't well at the time, and I didn't want to get involved in an argument with a man who obviously was very fanatical in his position. In his book he makes the statement that I was *unable* to answer his question. If he misquotes the other Bible expositors as he misquotes me, I would have no confidence in his book whatsoever.

In his book he maintains that the premillennial futurist viewpoint is something that is brand new. I'll admit that it has been fully developed, as have all these other interpretations, during the past few years. When I was a young man and a new Christian, I was introduced to the theory known as postmillennialism. The postmillennialists believed that the world would get better and better, that the church would convert the whole world, and then Christ would come and reign. Well, that viewpoint is almost dead today. After two world wars, a worldwide depression, and the crises through which the world is passing, there are very few who still hold that viewpoint. By the time I enrolled in the seminary of my denomination, every professor was an amillennialist, that is, they didn't believe in a millennium. It was to that view that most of the postmillennialists ran for cover. There was one professor in the seminary who was still a postmillennialist. He was very old and hard of hearing. In fact, when they told him that the war was over, he thought they meant the Civil War. He was really a back number, and he was still a postmillennialist.

At the risk of being a little tedious, I am going to give you the viewpoints of many men in the past to demonstrate that they were looking for Christ to return. They were not looking for the Great Tribulation, they were not even looking for the Millennium, but they were looking for Him to come. This expectation is the very heart of the premillennial viewpoint as we hold it today.

Barnabas, who was a co-worker with the apostle Paul, has been quoted as saying, "The true Sabbath is the one thousand years when Christ comes back to reign."

Clement (A.D. 96), Bishop of Rome, said, "Let us every hour expect the kingdom of God . . . we know not the day."

Polycarp (A.D. 108), Bishop of Smyrna and finally burned at the stake there, said, "He will raise us from the dead . . . we shall . . . reign with Him."

Ignatius, Bishop of Antioch, who the historian Eusebius says was the apostle Peter's successor, commented, "Consider the times and expect Him."

Papias (A.D. 116), Bishop of Hierapolis, who—according to Irenaeus—saw and heard the apostle John, said, "There will be one thousand years . . . when the reign of Christ personally will be established on earth."

Justin Martyr (A.D. 150) said, "I and all others who are orthodox Christians, on all points, know there will be a thousand years in Jerusalem . . . as Isaiah and Ezekiel declared."

Irenaeus (A.D. 175), Bishop of Lyons, commenting on Jesus' promise to drink again of the fruit of the vine in His Father's kingdom, argues: "That this . . . can only be fulfilled upon our Lord's personal return to earth."

Tertullian (A.D. 200) said, "We do indeed confess that a kingdom is promised on earth."

Martin Luther said, "Let us not think that the coming of Christ is far off."

John Calvin, in his third book of *Institutes*, wrote: "Scripture uniformly enjoins us to look with expectation for the advent of Christ."

Canon A. R. Fausset said this: "The early Christian fathers, Clement, Ignatius, Justin Martyr, and Irenaeus, looked for the Lord's speedy return as the necessary precursor of the millennial kingdom. Not until the professing Church lost her first love, and became the harlot resting on the world power, did she cease to be the Bride going forth to meet the Bridegroom, and seek to reign already on earth without waiting for His Advent."

Dr. Elliott wrote: "All primitive expositors, except Origen and the few who rejected Revelation, were premillennial."

Gussler's work on church history says of this blessed hope that "it was so distinctly and prominently mentioned that we do not hesitate in regarding it as the general belief of that age."

Chillingworth declared: "It was the doctrine believed and taught by the most eminent fathers of the age next to the apostles and by none of that age condemned."

Dr. Adolf von Harnack wrote: "The earlier fathers—Irenaeus, Hippolytus, Tertullian, etc.—believed it because it was part of the tradition of the early church. It is the same all through the third and fourth centuries with those Latin theologians who escaped the influence of Greek speculation."

My friend, I have quoted these many men of the past as proof of the fact that from the days of the apostles and through the church of the first centuries the interpretation of the Scriptures was premillennial. When someone makes the statement that premillennialism is something that originated one hundred years ago with an old witch in England, he doesn't know what he is talking about. It is interesting to note that premillennialism was the belief of these very outstanding men of the early church.

There are six striking and singular features about the Book of Revelation.

1. It is the only prophetic book in the New Testament. There are seventeen prophetic books in the Old Testament and only this one in the New Testament.

2. John, the writer, reaches farther back into eternity past than does any other writer in Scripture. He does this in his Gospel which opens with this: "In the beginning was the Word, and the Word was with God, and the Word was God" (John 1:1). Then he moves up to the time of creation: "All things were made by him; and without him was not any thing made that was made" (John 1:3). Then, when John writes the Book of Revelation, he reaches farther on into eternity future and the eternal kingdom of our Lord and Savior Jesus Christ.

3. There is a special blessing which is promised to the readers of this book: "Blessed is he that readeth, and they that hear the words of this prophecy, and keep those things which are written therein: for the time is at hand" (Rev. 1:3). It is a blessing promise. Also, there is a

warning given at the end of the book issued to those who tamper with its contents: "For I testify unto every man that heareth the words of the prophecy of this book, If any man shall add unto these things, God shall add unto him the plagues that are written in this book: and if any man shall take away from the words of the book of this prophecy, God shall take away his part out of the book of life, and out of the holy city, and from the things which are written in this book" (Rev. 22:18–19). That warning ought to make these wild and weird interpreters of prophecy stop, look, and listen. It is dangerous to say just *anything* relative to the Book of Revelation because people today realize that we have come to a great crisis in history. To say something that is entirely out of line is to mislead them. Unfortunately, the most popular prophetic teachers in our day are those who have gone out on a limb. This has raised a very serious problem, and later on we will have repercussions from it.

4. It is not a *sealed* book. Daniel was told to seal the book until the time of the end (see Dan. 12:9), but John is told: "Seal not the sayings of the prophecy of this book: for the time is at hand" (Rev. 22:10). To say that the Book of Revelation is a jumble and impossible to make heads or tails out of and cannot be understood is to contradict this. It is not a sealed book. In fact, it is probably the best organized book in the Bible.

5. It is a series of visions expressed in symbols which deal with *reality*. The literal interpretation is always preferred unless John makes it clear that it is otherwise.

6. It is like a great union station where the great trunk lines of prophecy have come in from other portions of Scripture. Revelation does not originate or begin anything. Rather it consummates and concludes that which has been begun somewhere else in Scripture. It is imperative to a right understanding of the book to be able to trace each great subject of prophecy from the first reference to the terminal. There are at least ten great subjects of prophecy which find their consummation here. This is the reason that a knowledge of the rest of the Bible is imperative to an understanding of the Book of Revelation. It is calculated that there are over five hundred references or allusions to

the Old Testament in Revelation and that, of its 404 verses, 278 contain references to the Old Testament. In other words, over half of this book depends upon your understanding of the Old Testament.

Let's look at the Book of Revelation as an airport with ten great airlines coming into it. We need to understand where each began and how it was developed as it comes into the Book of Revelation. The ten great subjects of prophecy which find their consummation here are these:

1. The Lord Jesus Christ. He is the subject of the book. The subject is not the beasts nor the bowls of wrath but the Sin-bearer. The first mention of Him is way back in Genesis 3:15, as the Seed of the woman.

2. The church does not begin in the Old Testament. It is first mentioned by the Lord Jesus in Matthew 16:18: "And I say also unto thee, That thou art Peter, and upon this rock I will build my church; and the gates of hell shall not prevail against it."

3. The resurrection and the translation of the saints (see John 14; 1 Thess. 4:13–18; 1 Cor. 15:51–52).

4. The Great Tribulation, spoken of back in Deuteronomy 4 where God says that His people would be in tribulation.

5. Satan and evil (see Ezek. 28:11–18).

6 The "man of sin" (see Ezek. 28:1–10).

7. The course and end of apostate Christendom (see Dan. 2·31–45; Matt. 13).

8. The beginning, course, and end of the "times of the Gentiles" (see Dan. 2:37–45; Luke 21:24). The Lord Jesus said that Jerusalem will be trodden down of the Gentiles until the Times of the Gentiles are fulfilled.

9. The second coming of Christ. According to Jude 14–15, Enoch spoke of that, which takes us back to the time of the Genesis record.

10. Israel's covenants, beginning with the covenant which God made with Abraham in Genesis 12:1–3. God promised Israel five things, and God says in Revelation that He will fulfill them all.

Now I want to make a positive statement: The Book of Revelation is not a difficult book. The liberal theologian has tried to make it a difficult book, and the amillennialist considers it a symbolic and hard-to-understand book. Even some of our premillennialists are trying to demonstrate that it is weird and wild.

Actually, it is the most orderly book in the Bible. And there is no reason to misunderstand it. This is what I mean: It divides itself. John puts down the instructions given to him by Christ: "Write the things which thou hast seen, and the things which are, and the things which shall be hereafter" (Rev. 1:19)—past, present, and future. Then we will find that the book further divides itself in series of sevens, and each division is as orderly as it possibly can be. You will find no other book in the Bible that divides itself like that.

To those who claim that it is all symbolic and beyond our understanding, I say that the Book of Revelation is to be taken literally. And when a symbol is used, it will be so stated. Also it will be symbolic of *reality*, and the reality will be more real than the symbol for the simple reason that John uses symbols to describe reality. In our study of the book, that is an all-important principle to follow. Let's allow the Revelation to say what it wants to say.

Therefore, we have no right to reach into the book and draw out of it some of the wonderful pictures that John describes for us and interpret them as taking place in our day. Some of them are symbolic, symbolic of reality, but not of a reality which is currently taking place.

The church is set before us in the figure of seven churches which were real churches in existence in John's day I have visited the ruins of all seven of them and have spent many hours there. In fact, I have visited some of them on four occasions, and I would love to go back tomorrow. To examine the ruins and study the locality is a very wonderful experience. It has made these churches live for me, and I can see how John was speaking into local situations but also giving the history of the church as a whole

Then after chapter 3, the church is not mentioned anymore The church is not the subject again in the entire Book of the Revelation. You may ask, "Do you mean that the church goes out of business?" Well, it leaves the earth and goes to heaven, and there it appears as the bride of Christ. When we see her in the last part of Revelation, she is not the church but the bride

Then beginning with chapter 4, everything is definitely in the future from our vantage point at the present time. So when anyone reaches in and pulls out a revelation—some vision about famine or wars or anything of that sort—it just does not fit into the picture of our day. We need to let John tell it like it is. In fact, we need to let the whole Bible speak to us like that—just let it say what it wants to say. The idea of making wild and weird interpretations is one of the reasons I enter this book with a feeling of fear.

It is interesting to note that the subject of prophecy is being developed in our day. The great doctrines of the church have been developed in certain historical periods. At first, it was the doctrine of the Scripture being the Word of God. This was followed by the doctrine of the person of Christ, known as Christology. Then the doctrine of soteriology, or salvation, was developed. And so it has been down through the years. Now you and I are living in a day when prophecy is really being developed, and we need to exercise care as to what and to whom we listen.

When the Pilgrims sailed for America, their pastor at Leyden reminded them, "The Lord has more truth yet to break forth from His Holy Word. . . . Luther and Calvin were great shining lights in their times, yet they penetrated not the whole counsel of God. . . . Be ready to receive whatever truth shall be made known to you from the written word of God." That, my friend, is very good advice because God is not revealing His truth by giving you a vision or a dream or a new religion. Therefore, we need to be very sure that all new truth comes from a correct interpretation of the Word of God.

As I have indicated, the twentieth century has witnessed a renewed interest in eschatology (the doctrine of last things) which we call prophecy. Especially since World War I, great strides have been made in this field. New light has fallen upon this phase of Scripture. All of this attention has focused the light of deeper study on the Book of Revelation.

In the notes which I have made on this book, I have attempted to avoid the pitfall of presenting something new and novel just for the sake of being different. Likewise, I have steered clear of repeating threadbare clichés. Many works on Revelation are merely carbon copies of other works. In my own library I have more commentaries on the Revelation than on any other book of the Bible, and most of them are almost *copies* of those that have preceded them.

Another danger we need to avoid is that of thinking that the Book of Revelation can be put on a chart. Although I myself have a chart and have used it in teaching, I will not be using it in this study. The reason is that if it includes all it should, it is so complicated that nobody will understand it. On the other hand, if it is so brief that it can be understood, it doesn't give enough information. I have several charts sent to me by different men in whom I have great confidence. One of them is so complicated that I need a chart to understand his chart! So, although I won't be using a chart, I will use the brief sketch below to attempt to simplify the different stages of the Revelation and also give the overall picture.

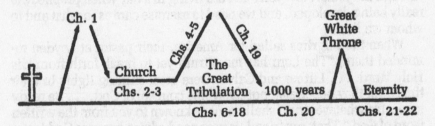

As you can see, it begins with the cross of Christ and His ascension. In chapter 1, we see the glorified Christ. In chapters 2—3 we see the church. In chapters 4—5 we see that the church is in heaven. Then on earth the Great Tribulation takes place, chapters 6—18. In chapter 19 we see that Christ returns to the earth and establishes His kingdom, and chapter 20 gives us the thousand-year reign of Christ. Then the Great White Throne is set up, the place where the lost are judged, and in chapters 21—22 eternity begins. That is the Book of Revelation.

Stauffer has made an important observation:

Domitian was also the first emperor to wage a proper campaign against Christ, and the church answered the attack under the leadership of Christ's last apostle, John of the Apocalypse. Nero had Paul and Peter destroyed, but he looked upon them as seditious Jews. Domitian was the first emperor to understand that behind the Christian movement there stood an enigmatic figure who threatened the glory of the emperors. He was the first to declare war on this figure, and the first also to lose the war—a foretaste of things to come.

The subject of this book is very important to see. To emphasize and reemphasize it, let me direct your attention to chapter 1, verse 1— "The Revelation of *Jesus Christ*, which God gave unto him, to shew unto his servants things which must shortly come to pass" (italics mine). Let's keep in mind that this book is a revelation of Jesus Christ. In the Gospels you see Him in the days of His flesh, but they do not give the full revelation of Jesus Christ. There you see Him in humiliation. Here in Revelation you see Him in glory. You see Him in charge of everything that takes place. He is in full command. This is the unveiling of Jesus Christ.

Snell has put it so well that I would like to quote him:

> In the Revelation the Lamb is the center around which all else is clustered, the foundation upon which everything lasting is built, the nail on which all hangs, the object to which all points, and the spring from which all blessing proceeds. The Lamb is the light, the glory, the life, the Lord of heaven and earth, from whose face all defilement must flee away, and in whose presence fullness of joy is known. Hence we cannot go far in the study of the Revelation without seeing the Lamb. Like direction posts along the road to remind us that He, who did by Himself purge our sins, is now highly exalted and that to Him every knee must bow and every tongue confess.

To that grand statement I say hallelujah! For the Lamb is going to reign upon this earth. That is God's intention, and that is God's purpose.

As I have said, the Book of Revelation is not really a difficult book it divides itself very easily. This is one book that doesn't require our labor in making divisions in it. John does it all for us according to the instructions given to him. In verse 18 of the first chapter the Lord Jesus speaks as the glorified Christ: "I am he that liveth, and was dead; and, behold, I am alive for evermore, Amen; and have the keys of hell and of death." Notice the four grand statements He makes concerning Himself: "I am alive. I was dead. I am alive for evermore. And I have the keys of hell [the grave] and of death." Then He tells John to write, and He gives him his outline in chapter 1, verse 19: "Write the things which thou hast seen, and the things which are, and the things which shall be hereafter." My friend, this is a wonderful, grand division that He is giving. In fact, there is nothing quite like it.

He first says, "I am he that liveth." And He instructs John, "Write the things which thou hast seen." That is past tense, referring to the vision of the Son of Man in heaven, the glorified Christ in chapter 1.

Then He says, "I was dead, and, behold, I am alive." And His instruction is, "Write the things which are." This is present tense, referring to Christ's present ministry. We are going to see that the living Christ is very busy doing things today. Do you realize that He is the Head of the church? Do you know the reason the contemporary church is in such a mess? The reason is that the church is like a body that has been decapitated. It is no longer in touch with the Head of the church. We will see Christ's ministry to the church in chapters 2—3.

Thirdly, Christ said, "I have the keys of hell and of death." And when we get to chapter 5, we will see that no one could be found to open the book but one—the Lord Jesus Christ. So chapters 4—22 deal with the future, and Christ said to John, "Write the things that you are about to see after these things." It is very important to see that "after these things" is the Greek *meta tauta*. After what things? After the church things. So in chapters 4—22 he is dealing with things that are going to take place after the church leaves the earth The fallacy of the hour is reaching into this third section and trying to pull those events up to the present. This gives rise to the wild and weird interpretations we hear in our day. Why don't we follow what John tells us? He gives us the past, present, and future of the Book of Revelation. He will let us know when he gets to the *meta tauta*, the "after these things." You can't miss it—unless you follow a system of interpretation that doesn't fit into the Book of Revelation.

As you will see by the outline that follows, I have used the divisions which John has given to us:

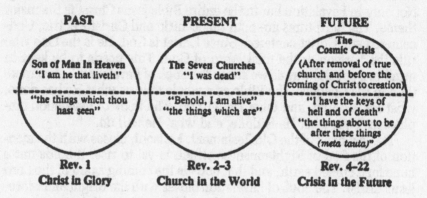

PAST	PRESENT	FUTURE

PAST

Son of Man In Heaven
"I am he that liveth"

"the things which thou
hast seen"

Rev. 1
Christ in Glory

PRESENT

The Seven Churches
"I was dead"

"Behold, I am alive"
"the things which are"

Rev. 2–3
Church in the World

FUTURE

The
Cosmic Crisis
(After removal of true
church and before the
coming of Christ to creation)

"I have the keys of
hell and of death"
"the things about to be
after these things
(meta tauta)"

Rev. 4–22
Crisis in the Future

I. The *Person* of Jesus Christ—Christ in glory, chapter 1.
II. The *Possession* of Jesus Christ—the church in the world is His, chapters 2—3.
III. The *Program* of Jesus Christ—as seen in heaven, chapters 4—22.

The last section deals with the consummation of all things on this earth. This is what makes Revelation such a glorious and wonderful book.

In the first division of the Book of Revelation we will see the person of Christ in His position and glory as the Great High Priest who is in charge of His church. We will see that He is in absolute control. In the Gospels we find Him to be meek, lowly, and humble. He made Himself subject to His enemies on earth and died upon a cross! We find a completely different picture of Him in the Book of the Revelation. Here He is in absolute control. Although He is still the *Lamb* of God, it is His wrath that is revealed, the wrath of the Lamb, and it terrifies the earth. When He speaks in wrath, His judgment begins upon the earth.

The person of Jesus Christ is the theme of this book. When the scene moves to heaven, we see Him there, too, controlling everything. Not only in Revelation but in the entire Bible Jesus Christ is the major theme. The Scriptures are both theocentric and Christocentric, God-centered and Christ-centered. Since Christ is God, He is the One who fills the horizon of the total Word of God. This needs to be kept in mind in a special way as we study the Book of Revelation—even more than in the Gospels. The Bible as a whole tells us what He has done, what He is doing, and what He will do. The Book of Revelation emphasizes both what He is doing and what He will do.

The last book of the Old Testament, Malachi, closes with the mention of the Son of Righteousness which is yet to rise. It holds out a hope for a cursed earth, and that hope is the coming again of the Lord Jesus Christ. The Book of Revelation closes with the Bright and Morning Star, which is a figure of Christ at His coming to take the church out of the world. The Rapture is the hope of the New Testament, just as the revelation of Christ was the hope of the Old Testament. And the Book of Revelation will complete the revelation of Christ.

Notice also that there is a tie between Genesis and Revelation, the first and last books of the Bible. Genesis presents the beginning, and Revelation presents the end. Note the contrasts between the two books:

In Genesis the earth was created; in Revelation the earth passes away.

In Genesis was Satan's first rebellion; in Revelation is Satan's last rebellion.

In Genesis the sun, moon, and stars were for earth's government; in Revelation these same heavenly bodies are for earth's judgment. In Genesis the sun was to govern the day; in Revelation there is no need of the sun.

In Genesis darkness was called night; in Revelation there is "no night there" (see Rev. 21:25; 22:5).

In Genesis the waters were called seas; in Revelation there is no more sea.

In Genesis was the entrance of sin; in Revelation is the exodus of sin.

In Genesis the curse was pronounced; in Revelation the curse is removed.

In Genesis death entered; in Revelation there is no more death.

In Genesis was the beginning of sorrow and suffering; in Revelation there will be no more sorrow and no more tears.

In Genesis was the marriage of the first Adam; in Revelation is the marriage of the Last Adam.

In Genesis we saw man's city, Babylon, being built; in Revelation we see man's city, Babylon, destroyed and God's city, the New Jerusalem, brought into view.

In Genesis Satan's doom was pronounced; in Revelation Satan's doom is executed.

It is interesting that Genesis opens the Bible not only with a global view but also with a universal view—"In the beginning God created the heaven and the earth" (Gen. 1:1). And the Bible closes with another global and universal book. The Revelation shows what God is going to do with His universe and with His creatures. There is no other book quite like this.

OUTLINE

I. **The Person of Jesus Christ—Christ in Glory, Chapter 1**
   A. Title of the Book, Chapter 1:1
   B. Method of Revelation, Chapter 1:2
   C. Beatitude of Bible Study, Chapter 1:3
   D. Greetings from John the Writer and from Jesus Christ in Heaven, Chapter 1:4–8
   E. The Post-Incarnate Christ in a Glorified Body, Judging His Church (the Great High Priest in the Holy of Holies), Chapter 1:9–18
      "we know him no longer after the flesh"
   F. Time Division of the Contents of Apocalypse, Chapter 1:19
   G. Interpretation of the Seven Stars and Seven Lampstands, Chapter 1:20

II. **The Possession of Jesus Christ—The Church in the World, Chapters 2—3**
   A. Letter of Christ to the Church in Ephesus, Chapter 2:1–7
   B. Letter of Christ to the Church in Smyrna, Chapter 2:8–11
   C. Letter of Christ to the Church in Pergamum, Chapter 2:12–17
   D. Letter of Christ to the Church in Thyatira, Chapter 2:18–29
   E. Letter of Christ to the Church in Sardis, Chapter 3:1–6
   F. Letter of Christ to the Church in Philadelphia, Chapter 3:7–13
   G. Letter of Christ to the Church in Laodicea, Chapter 3:14–22

III. **The Program of Jesus Christ—The Scene in Heaven, Chapters 4—22**
   A. The Church in Heaven with Christ, Chapters 4—5
      "I will come again, and receive you unto myself; that where I am there ye may be also"
      1. Throne of God, Chapter 4:1–3
      2. Twenty-four Elders, Chapter 4:4–5

CHAPTER 1

THEME: The person of Jesus Christ

In the first division of this book we see the person of Christ. We see Christ in His glory and position as the Great High Priest who is in charge of His church. We see Him in absolute control. In the Gospels we find Him meek, lowly, humble, and dying upon a cross. He made Himself subject to His enemies on earth. He is not like that in the Book of Revelation. He is in control. He is still the Lamb of God, but we see the wrath of the Lamb that terrifies the earth.

The major theme of the entire Bible is the Lord Jesus Christ. The Scriptures are both theocentric and Christocentric. Since Christ is God, He is the One who fills the horizon of the total Word of God. This needs to be kept in mind in the Book of Revelation more than in any other book of the Bible, even more than in the Gospels. The Bible tells what He has done, is doing, and will do. Revelation emphasizes what He is doing and what He will do. We need to keep that in mind.

THE TITLE OF THE BOOK

The Revelation of Jesus Christ, which God gave unto him, to shew unto his servants things which must shortly come to pass; and he sent and signified it by his angel unto his servant John [Rev. 1:1].

In my book *Reveling Through Revelation* I have included my own literal translation of each verse of the Book of Revelation, and in this book I will use some of it also. I don't use it because it is better. For many years I have called my translation the McGee-icus Ad Absurdum translation. I would not defend it if anyone made an attack upon it. It is merely an attempt to lift out of the Greek what John is actually saying and to try to couch it in language that may be a little more literal

and understandable to us in our day. It will appear in italicized type
after the King James version:

> *The unveiling of Jesus Christ which God gave Him to
> show unto His bond servants things which must shortly
> come to pass completely, and He sent and signified it
> (gave a sign) by His angel (messenger) to His servant
> John.*

First of all, please note that the title of this book is Revelation—
singular, not plural. A retired preacher came to me when I was a pastor in downtown Los Angeles to make an attack upon my
interpretation of the Book of Revelation. He said, "You just don't know
anything about Revelations," using the plural. I replied, "Brother, you
are absolutely accurate in that I know nothing about the Book of Revelations. I have never even seen that book." He was astounded and later
embarrassed by his own ignorance when he realized that the Book of
Revelation is the Revelation. It is the *apokalupsis*, that is, "the uncov-
ering, unveiling, or revelation" of Jesus Christ.

"To shew unto his servants things which must shortly come to
pass." In the last chapter of Revelation, John is instructed, "Seal not
the sayings of the prophecy of this book: for the time is at hand" (Rev.
22:10). It is not a sealed book; it is open and to be understood in our
day. This is in contrast to the prophecy in the Book of Daniel which
Daniel was instructed to seal. Our Lord Jesus gave what are known as
the "mystery" parables. Very frankly, to the majority of the church
today they are still a mystery. But our Lord put it like this: "And he
said unto them, Unto you it is given to know the mystery of the kingdom of God: but unto them that are without, all these things are done
in parables: that seeing they may see, and not perceive; and hearing
they may hear, and not understand; lest at any time they should be
converted, and their sins should be forgiven them" (Mark 4:11–12).
You see, my friend, in the Gospels we have only the half-story. We
need the Book of Revelation because it is the consummation of it. Of
course, it can be understood only if the Spirit of God is our teacher.
But the Book of Revleation takes off the veil so we can see Christ in His

unveiled beauty and power and glory. This book is the opposite of a secret or a mystery. It is a disclosure of secrets, and it is called prophecy in the next verse, as we shall see.

When a so-called Christian says that he does not understand the Book of Revelation, it makes me wonder, because this book was given to us in order that we might understand these mysteries of the kingdom of God.

"To show" means by word pictures, by symbols, by direct and indirect representations.

"And he sent and signified it." That is, he used symbols. And keep in mind that the symbols are symbolic of reality. Peter gave us a great rule for the interpretation of prophecy in 2 Peter 1:20: "Knowing this first, that no prophecy of the scripture is of any private interpretation." You don't interpret a single text by itself; you interpret it in the light of the entire Word of God. Ottman said, "The figurative language of Revelation is figurative of facts."

"To shew . . . things" assures us that what John tells us is not ethereal and ephemeral dream stuff. There is a hard core of real facts in this book. What are "things"? One night Mrs. McGee and I took care of our little grandson. We let him play in the den where we keep a bunch of toys for him to play with when he stays with us. He went into the den and got out all of those things. In fact, he calls them his things. He spread them all over the floor of the den. We indulge the little fellow, and we didn't make him pick up all of his toys after he was through playing. We didn't pick them up either. So later that night, when I walked through the den, I stepped on some of his things. In fact, I stumbled over them and took a tumble. You can say that "things" are symbols, but you don't take a tumble over symbols. And in the Book of Revelation, the "things" are made out of hard stuff. These "things" are reality. Any time John uses a symbol, he will make it clear to us that he is using a symbol. And we can be sure that he is using a symbol because the reality is far greater than the symbol. In fact, the symbol is a poor representation of the reality.

"Must"—He says that they must shortly come to pass. The word must has in it an urgent necessity and an absolute certainty.

"Shortly" has a connotation that is very important for us to note.

The word occurs quite a few times in the Scriptures. For instance, we have it in Luke 18:8 where our Lord says, "I tell you that he will avenge them [His elect] speedily. . " The word *speedily* is the same word as *shortly*. It means that when the vengeance begins, it will take place in a hurry. There will be no waiting around for it. That implies that the Lord is not coming soon, but that when He does return, the things He is talking about will happen shortly and with great speed His vengeance will take place in a brief period of time.

John tells us that it is the revelation of Jesus Christ which *God* gave to Him. Notice the steps of revelation:

THE STEPS OF REVELATION

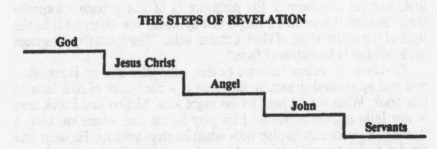

It originated with God, it was given to Jesus Christ, He gave it to His angel, His angel gave it to John, and from John it goes to His servants that they might know what is coming to pass. And that is the way it has come to you and me today.

By the way, this raises a question that I sometimes hear. Someone says, "Well, preacher, you painted yourself into a corner, because you said that angels are not connected with the church age." Yes, and I still say that. The angel mentioned here is a heavenly messenger, but notice that John is writing primarily about future things; that is, what Jesus is going to do in the future. And beginning with chapter 4, everything is future and will take place after the church has left the earth. Therefore, we see angels coming back into prominence. This is true to the way the book moves.

THE METHOD OF REVELATION

Who bare record of the word of God, and of the testimony of Jesus Christ, and of all things that he saw [Rev. 1:2].

Who bore witness of the Word of God, and of the testimony (witness) of Jesus Christ, even as many things as he saw.

"Who bare record" or, as I have translated it, "who bore witness" is in the Greek an epistolary aorist. It means that John projects himself up to where his readers are, where you and I are in this day, and he looks back at what he is writing.

"Of the word of God." The "word of God" refers, I believe, to both Christ and the contents of this book. He is the living Word, and when the written Word reveals Him to us, He is the living Word, you may be sure of that.

"And of the testimony [witness] of Jesus Christ." I prefer the word *witness* rather than *testimony*. It occurs ninety times in the writings of John—fifty times in his Gospel record.

"And of all things that he saw." He was an eyewitness of the visions. What John saw, he made pictures of, and the Book of Revelation is television, friend. It was the first television program ever presented, and it is one you would do well to watch. It came from heaven from God the Father, through His Son, Jesus Christ, and it was given to an angel who gave it to John, who wrote about what he saw. Not only did John hear, he also saw, and these are the two avenues through which we get most of our information. I sometimes wonder if John didn't smell things just a little bit, too, because there are parts of this book where you catch the odor also.

THE BEATITUDE OF BIBLE STUDY

Blessed is he that readeth, and they that hear the words of this prophecy, and keep those things which are written therein: for the time is at hand [Rev. 1:3].

This verse gives us the beatitude of Bible study. This is the first of seven *beatitudes* found in the Book of Revelation. This verse says, "Blessed is he that readeth," and that means the reader, or in the church, the teacher. Both those who read this book and those who hear it will be blessed. And both the reader and the hearer are to keep those things which are written in the book. The threefold blessing comes from reading, hearing, and keeping. I believe those who go through the Book of Revelation will receive a special blessing. I really believe it because that is what John says.

"For the time is at hand" does not mean that the things which are mentioned at the end of the book are happening in our day, but it does mean that the beginning of the church on the Day of Pentecost began this movement of the Lord Jesus' ministry in heaven. We are going to see a vision of Him in this chapter, a vision of the glorified Christ. Then we will see what His ministry is, and that will move us right on into the future.

GREETINGS FROM JOHN, THE WRITER, AND FROM CHRIST IN HEAVEN

John to the seven churches which are in Asia: Grace be unto you, and peace, from him which is, and which was, and which is to come; and from the seven Spirits which are before his throne [Rev. 1:4].

This is a very wonderful greeting! "John to the seven churches which are in Asia." "Asia" encompassed a great deal of what we generally call Asia Minor or modern Turkey. Notice that John connects no title with his name. I have a notion that John was well known in these seven churches. We know that he had been pastor of the church at Ephesus, and apparently he had oversight of all the churches in that area.

Before we go further, let me call your attention to the number seven. In this verse there is the mention of seven churches and seven Spirits. The number seven has a religious meaning in the Word of God, which was apparent to the people in John's day but is totally foreign to us in our day. The gambling sector of our society is very conscious of numbers, as are folk who are superstitious, but we are not accustomed to attaching any religious significance to numbers. However, in the Word of God the number seven is prominent. It does not denote perfection, but it does denote completeness. Sometimes completeness is perfection, but not always.

Seven speaks of that which is complete and that which is representative. In a particular way, seven has to do with God's covenant and dealings with Israel. For instance, the Sabbath, circumcision, and worship are all hinged around the seventh day. As you go through the Word of God, you notice that Jericho was compassed about seven times. Naaman was instructed to dip in the Jordan River seven times, there were seven years of plenty and seven years of famine in Joseph's time in Egypt, Nebuchadnezzar was insane for seven years, there are seven beatitudes in the New Testament, there are seven petitions in the Lord's Prayer, there are seven parables in Matthew 13, seven loaves fed the multitude, Jesus spoke seven times from the cross, and in the Book of Revelation the number seven cannot be ignored or considered accidental. Seven is the key number of this book.

Here in the fourth verse, John writes to the "seven churches." Weren't there other churches in Asia? We know there were churches at Colosse, Miletus, Hierapolis, Troas, and at many other places. I have stayed at Hierapolis. It is still a place, and it is about ten miles from Laodicea, which is now in ruins. There are three motels at Laodicea and a store or two. The ruins of Hierapolis are absolutely magnificent and quite significant, because they reveal what a tremendous place it was at one time. In contrast, the ruins of Laodicea are, for the most part, under a wild oat field. They have not been excavated. John was directed to write to seven churches, and Hierapolis was not one of the seven, although it was an important center of Christian influence and the ruins of four early Christian churches have been found there. John was directed to write to only seven certain churches because he was giving the complete history of the church and they were representative churches, as we shall see.

"Asia" refers to the provinces which include Lydia, Mysia, Caria, and parts of Phrygia. It does not mean the continent of Asia nor does it include all of Asia Minor (Asia Minor is a term which was not used until the fourth century A.D.), but it covers a great area of Asia Minor, especially along the coast.

"Grace be unto you, and peace." The word *grace* is *charis*, the Greek form of greeting, and *peace* is *shalom*, the Hebrew form of greeting. Peace flows from grace, and grace is the source of all our blessings today. The Book of Revelation reveals the grace of God and also peace. We don't need to be frightened as we study this book; we can have the peace of God in our hearts.

It is "from him . . . and from the seven Spirits," which brings the Trinity before us. The "seven Spirits" refer to the Holy Spirit and probably have reference to the seven branches of the lampstand, as we shall see later on.

"Which is, and which was, and which is to come" emphasizes the eternity and immutability of God. Notice now the mention of each member of the Trinity: "Jesus Christ" (in the next verse) refers to God the Son, the "seven Spirits" refer to the Holy Spirit, and "him which is, and which was, and which is to come" refers to God the Father.

> **And from Jesus Christ, who is the faithful witness, and the first begotten of the dead, and the prince of the kings of the earth. Unto him that loved us, and washed us from our sins in his own blood,**
>
> **And hath made us kings and priests unto God and his Father; to him be glory and dominion for ever and ever. Amen [Rev. 1:5–6].**

In these two verses we have the titles which are given to the Lord Jesus Christ, and the interesting thing is that there are seven titles:

1. "Faithful witness"—Jesus Christ is the only trustworthy witness to the facts of this book. The facts are about Him. He testifies of Himself. It is difficult to believe other people, but we can believe the Lord Jesus.

2. "First begotten of the dead" is firstborn from the dead. First-born is the Greek *prototokos*, which has to do with resurrection. He is

the first to rise from the dead, never to die again. This is a marvelous picture! Death was a womb which bore Him. He came out of death into life. The tomb was a womb, as far as He was concerned. He is the only One back from the dead in a glorified body. No one else has come that route yet, but His own are going to follow Him in resurrection, and the Rapture will be next (see 1 Thess. 4:14). Then will come the revelation when He will come to the earth.

3. "The prince [ruler] of the kings of the earth" speaks of His ultimate position during the Millennium. "Wherefore God also hath highly exalted him, and given him a name which is above every name: That at the name of Jesus every knee should bow, of things in heaven, and things in earth, and things under the earth; And that every tongue should confess that Jesus Christ is Lord, to the glory of God the Father" (Phil. 2:9–11).

4. "Unto him that loved us" is actually in the present tense and emphasizes His constant attitude toward His own. The Book of Revelation should not frighten us too much because of the fact that it is from the One who loves us. Jesus Christ didn't love us only when He died on the cross, although He loved us at that time, but He also loves us today. Right at this very minute, Jesus loves you.

5. "Washed [loosed] us from our sins in his own blood." The blood of Christ is very important. It is not just a symbol. In the Old Testament, God taught His people that the ". . . life of the flesh is in the blood . . ." (Lev. 17:11). In this verse God goes on to say, "I have given it to you upon the altar to make an atonement for your souls. . . ." When Christ shed His blood, I think every drop came out of His body. He gave that for you and for me. He gave His life, if you please. He died, and I am not inclined to belittle the blood of Christ as some men are doing today. I still like the song with these words:

> There is a fountain filled with blood
> Drawn from Immanuel's veins;
> And sinners, plunged beneath that flood,
> Lose all their guilty stains.
> "There Is a Fountain"
> —William Cowper

Peter wrote, "Forasmuch as ye know that ye were not redeemed with corruptible things, as silver and gold, from your vain conversation received by tradition from your fathers; but with the precious blood of Christ, as of a lamb without blemish and without spot" (1 Pet. 1:18-19). Because of that shed blood, Paul could write to the young preacher Timothy, "For there is one God, and one mediator between God and men, the man Christ Jesus" (1 Tim. 2:5). He loosed us from our sins in His own blood. What a wonderful, glorious thing!

6. "And hath made us kings and priests [a kingdom of priests] unto God and his Father"—believers are never called kings. They are a kingdom of priests and are going to rule with the Lord Jesus. Quite frankly, I don't get wrought up over the popular song, "The King Is Coming." The King is coming, all right, but when He comes as King, He will come to the *earth*, and at that time He is going to put down all unrighteousness. But before He comes to earth as King, He will come in the air, an event we call the Rapture. At that time He will come as my Savior. He comes as the Bridegroom for His bride, the church, whom He loves and gave Himself for. He comes as the lover of my soul. For this reason I am not thrilled with "The King Is Coming." My relationship to Him is much closer. He is my Lord. He has not made us "kings and priests," He has made us a kingdom of priests, and we are going to reign with Him.

It is interesting to note that it reads, "unto God and *his* Father." Why doesn't it read, "unto God and our Father"? Because He is the Father of Jesus in a sense that He is not our Father. You see, we become sons of God through regeneration, being born from above, by accepting Him as Savior. But Christ's *eternal* position in the Trinity is that of the Son.

7. "To Him the glory and the dominion unto the ages of the ages" (my own translation). This is emphasizing eternity. "Amen." Christ is the amen, as we saw in Isaiah. That is a title for Him. Jesus Christ is both the subject and the object of this book. He is the mover of all events, and all events move toward Him. He is the far-off eternal purpose in everything. All things were not only made *by* Him, but all things were made *for* Him. This universe exists for Him.

Behold, he cometh with clouds; and every eye shall see
him, and they also which pierced him: and all kindreds
of the earth shall wail because of him. Even so, Amen
[Rev. 1:7].

"Behold, he cometh with clouds" denotes the personal and physical
coming of Christ.

"And every eye shall see him" reveals that His coming will be a
physical and bodily appearance, an appeal to the eye-gate. As far as
we know, when Christ takes the church out of the world at the Rapture, He doesn't appear to everyone. I don't believe in a secret rapture
as some folk have attempted to describe it, but at the time of the Rapture He does not come to the earth. Believers are to be caught up to
meet the Lord in the air. If Christ will be coming to the earth at that
time, there is no point in being caught up in the air. Therefore, this is
not the Rapture which is being described in this verse. This is His
return to the earth as King.

"Every eye shall see him." The emphasis in the Book of Revelation
is upon His coming to this earth to establish His kingdom.

"All kindreds of the earth shall wail because of him." Probably a
better translation is this: "All the tribes of the earth shall beat their
breasts because of him." This is going to be the reaction of all Christ-
rejectors. The world will not want to see Him.

"Even so, Amen" means "Yea, faithful." He is going to do it, my
friend. He is not going to change His mind about it. He is faithful.

I am Alpha and Omega, the beginning and the ending,
saith the Lord, which is, and which was, and which is
to come, the Almighty [Rev. 1:8].

"I am Alpha and Omega." This is quite a remarkable statement in the
Greek language. The alpha and omega are the first and last letters of
the Greek alphabet. From an alphabet you make words, and Jesus
Christ is called the "Word of God"—the full revelation and intelligent
communication of God. He is the only alphabet you can use to reach

God, my friend. The only language God speaks and understands is the language where Jesus is the Alpha and the Omega and all the letters in between. He is the "A" and the "Z," and He is the "ABC." If you are going to get through to God the Father, you will have to go through the Son, Jesus Christ. Here the emphasis is upon the beginning and the end. Here in the original Greek the Omega is not spelled out as is the Alpha. Why? Because Christ is the beginning, and the beginning is already completed. But the end is yet to be; so He didn't spell out the Omega in this instance. One day He will complete God's program. This is a very interesting detail in the Greek text.

"The beginning and the ending" refers to the eternity of the Son and His immutability. Concerning this, Hebrews 13:8 says, "Jesus Christ the same yesterday, and today, and for ever." When it says that He is the same, it does not mean that He is walking over yonder by the Sea of Galilee today. He is not. But it means that in His attributes He is the same. He has not changed. He is immutable. Since He is the beginning and the ending, He encompasses all time and eternity.

"Saith the Lord" is an affirmation of the deity of the Lord Jesus Christ.

"Which is," that is, at the present time, He is the glorified Christ.

"Which was"—past time, the first coming of Christ as Savior.

"Which is to come"—future time, the second coming of Christ as the Sovereign over this earth.

Verses 4–8 have comprised this very remarkable section of greetings from John, the writer, and from the Lord Jesus Christ. Remember that He says He loves us; so let's not be afraid of anything that is to follow.

THE POST-INCARNATE CHRIST IN A GLORIFIED BODY JUDGING HIS CHURCH

I John, who also am your brother, and companion in tribulation, and in the kingdom and patience of Jesus Christ, was in the isle that is called Patmos, for the word of God, and for the testimony of Jesus Christ [Rev. 1:9].

*I, John, who am your brother, and partaker with you in
the persecution (for Christ's sake), and kingdom and patience in Jesus; I was (found myself) in the isle called
Patmos because of [Gr.: dia, on account of] the Word of
God and the witness of Jesus.*

"I John" is used three times in this Book of Revelation—the other two
are at the end of the book.

"Your brother, and companion in tribulation" does not refer to the
Great Tribulation. John was in trouble. Domitian (A.D. 96), the Roman
emperor, had put him in prison on the Isle of Patmos. John had been
active in the church at Ephesus, and he had supervision over all the
other churches, and he had been teaching the Word of God. You get
into trouble when you teach all of the Word of God. John knew all
about trouble, and so did the early church. So if it comes to you and
me, it is nothing new at all.

Again let me say that John is not referring to the Great Tribulation
but to the persecution that was already befalling believers. And "the
kingdom" refers to the present state of the kingdom. By virtue of the
new birth, which places a sinner in Christ, he is likewise in the kingdom of God. This is not the millennial kingdom—that has not been
established yet. Christ will institute it at His coming.

Someone has said that we are living today in the kingdom and
patience—patience is where the emphasis is.

John explains the reason he was on the Isle of Patmos. He was exiled there from about A.D. 86 to 96. It is a rugged, volcanic island off
the coast of Asia Minor. It is about ten miles long and six miles wide.

"Jesus," you will notice, is the name used by John in both his Gospel and in the Apocalypse. When he wants to bring glory to Him, he
calls Him Jesus, and then he lifts Him to the skies. I hope that we can
do that, also.

Before we look at the next verses, let me remind you that John was
given this great vision on the lonely Isle of Patmos. It is a vision of the
post-incarnate Christ in His glorified body as He is judging His
church. In other words, we shall see the Great High Priest in the Holy
of Holies.

I was in the Spirit on the Lord's day, and heard behind me a great voice, as of a trumpet,

Saying, I am Alpha and Omega, the first and the last: and, What thou seest, write in a book, and send it unto the seven churches which are in Asia; unto Ephesus, and unto Smyrna, and unto Pergamos, and unto Thyatira, and unto Sardis, and unto Philadelphia, and unto Laodicea [Rev. 1:10–11].

I was (found myself) in (the) Spirit in the Lord's Day, and heard behind me a great sound, as of a (war) trumpet, saying, What you are seeing, write (promptly) into a book, and send (promptly) to the seven churches, unto Ephesus, and unto Smyrna, and unto Pergamos, and unto Thyatira, and unto Sardis, and unto Philadelphia, and unto Laodicea.

My own transition is not a finished translation by any means, and I do not recommend it, but it is an attempt to get from the original Greek what is actually being said.

The Holy Spirit is here performing His office work. That is why I pray that the Spirit of God might take the things of Christ and show them unto us. That is exactly what the Lord Jesus Christ said the Holy Spirit would do when He came. The Lord's exact words were, "Howbeit when he, the Spirit of truth, is come, he will guide you into all truth: for he shall not speak of himself; but whatsoever he shall hear, that shall he speak: and he will shew you things to come. He shall glorify me: for he shall receive of mine, and shall shew it unto you" (John 16:13–14).

We are beginning to get a vision of the glorified Christ. We are considering Him in His office as the Great High Priest today.

I fully recognize that in myself I am totally incompetent to try to explain these tremendous verses. Only the Spirit of God can make them real to us. However, Hebrews 3:1 tells us, "Wherefore, holy brethren, partakers of the heavenly calling, consider the Apostle and

High Priest of our profession, Christ Jesus." So we are considering Him in His present office of Great High Priest.

"I was in the Spirit," John says. The Holy Spirit was moving upon John and giving him a panoramic picture. This is cinerama. It is sight and sound. It is an appeal to both the eye-gate and the ear-gate.

"On the Lord's day." The meaning of this is controversial. Some outstanding scholars interpret this as being a reference to the Day of the Lord. While I certainly respect them and their viewpoint, I cannot accept this view, although the great theme of Revelation will deal with the Day of the Lord, which is the Tribulation Period and the millennial kingdom. But John says that he was in the Spirit on the Lord's Day and, in my judgment, the Day of the Lord and the Lord's Day are two different things. We recognize that anti-fat and fat auntie are two different things and that a chestnut horse and a horse chestnut are two different things. And I would say that the Day of the Lord and the Lord's Day are two different things also, and that the Lord's Day refers to what we call Sunday.

"I . . . heard behind me a great voice, as of a trumpet." Who was it? He will tell us—

> And I turned to see the voice that spake with me. And being turned, I saw seven golden candlesticks;
>
> And in the midst of the seven candlesticks one like unto the Son of man, clothed with a garment down to the foot, and girt about the paps with a golden girdle [Rev. 1:12-13].
>
> And I turned to see the voice which was speaking with me, and when I turned, I saw seven golden lampstands, and in the midst of the lampstands One like to a Son of Man, clothed with a garment, reaching to the foot, and girt about the breasts with a golden girdle.

John heard a voice like a war trumpet, and it spoke to him. When the Lord Jesus descends from heaven to remove His church from the earth, He will come with a shout. First Thessalonians 4:16 tells us about it: "For the Lord himself shall descend from heaven with a shout, with the voice of the archangel, and with the trump of God: and the dead in Christ shall rise first." His voice will be like the voice of an archangel, and His voice will be like a trumpet, because it is identified here as just that. But it will be Christ's own voice. He is not going to need any archangel to help Him raise His own from the dead.

What a thrill it is to see this picture of the Lord Jesus Christ! It is a vision of One like the Son of Man. He is "clothed with a garment down to the foot, and girt about the breast with a golden girdle." The seven golden lampstands remind us of the tabernacle. There it was one lampstand with seven branches. Here it is seven separate lampstands. Since these lampstands represent seven separate churches (v. 20), the difference is explained. The function of all is the same. The Lord Jesus said, "I am the light of the world, and when I leave, you are to be the light in the world" (see John 8:12).

We see the Lord Jesus Christ pictured here as our Great High Priest. His garments are those of the high priest—check Exodus 28:2–4. The garments represent the inherent righteousness of Christ. In Him is no sin, and He knew no sin.

Concerning the girdle, Josephus states that the priests were girded about the breasts. The ordinary custom was to be girded about the loins. But the emphasis here is not on service but on strength. It speaks of His judgment in truth.

We are asked to consider our Great High Priest as He stands in the midst of the churches. He is judging the churches; He is judging believers that the light might continue to shine. My friend, it is important to see what Christ's present ministry is.

This is a subject about which I have wanted to write. I haven't gotten around to it yet and may never write it, but I have a title for it: The Contemporary Christ. I hear so many foolish things that are being said about what Jesus is doing in our day. My friend, the Scripture does not leave us in the dark regarding what He is doing today. It mentions three very definite ministries.

First, there is the intercession of Christ. He is our Great High Priest. He is standing at the golden altar in heaven today, where He ever lives to make intercession for us (see Heb. 7:25). We love that part of His ministry. It is a wonderful thing.

Secondly, we have the *intervention* of Christ. He steps outside of the Holy Place to the laver. There He washes the feet of those who are His own. He washes those who have confessed their sins. Christians have sin, and those sins must be confessed in order to have fellowship with Him. "If we confess our sins, he is faithful and just to forgive us our sins, and to cleanse us from all unrighteousness" (1 John 1:9). He is girded today with the towel, and He carries the basin; He intervenes on our behalf.

John also says in his first epistle: "My little children, these things write I unto you, that ye sin not." He has made every provision that we sin not. I don't know about you, but I haven't reached that state yet. And, frankly, I have never met anyone who has. But John says, "And if any man sin, we have an advocate with the Father . . ." (1 John 2:1). Christ is our advocate. That is, He is on our side defending us when we are accused, and Satan is the accuser of the brethren.

There is yet another ministry of Christ that is not very popular. It is the ministry mentioned in the first chapter of Revelation, and I think that is one reason this section of Revelation is so little known. Here we see His ministry of *inspection*. What Christ is doing today is clearly outlined in the Scriptures. He ascended to heaven and sat down at the right hand of God, but He did not start twiddling His thumbs. When we are told that He "sat down," it means that He finished His work of redemption for man. He died on earth to save us, and He lives in heaven to keep us saved. I think He is busier today trying to keep us saved than He was when He was on earth.

We have the three ministries of Christ; we have His *intercession*, His *intervention*, and His *inspection*. The inspection of Christ is what we are going to look at now. Where is He now? We see Him walking in the midst of the lampstands. In the Book of Exodus we see the golden lampstand. It was the most beautiful article of furniture in the tabernacle. It was made of solid gold, and there were three branches on each side of the main stem. The top of each stem was fashioned like an open almond blossom, and the lamps were set there. The lamps represent the Holy Spirit; the golden lampstand itself represents Christ—

His glory and His deity. Christ sent the Holy Spirit into the world. The golden lampstand holds up the lamps, and the lamps, in turn, reveal the beauty and glory of the lampstand. That is the picture we have in Revelation. I trust that even now the Holy Spirit will make Christ, in all of His glory, wonder, and beauty, *real* to you that you may see yourself in the light of His presence as He inspects you. That is not a popular teaching today. We don't like to be inspected, but in Revelation we see Him walking in the midst of the lampstands, performing His ministry of inspection.

In the tabernacle the high priest had the sole oversight of the lampstand. The other priests had other duties to perform, but the high priest took care of the lampstand. He was the one who lighted the lamps. He poured in the oil and trimmed the wicks. If one of the lamps began to smoke and did not give a good clear light, he was the one who snuffed it out. The Lord Jesus is walking in the midst of the lampstands today. He is in the midst of His church, made up of individual believers. He is doing several things: He trims the wicks. In John 15 we are told that He prunes the branches of believers so that they might bring forth fruit. One of the reasons He lets us go through certain trials on earth is so that He might get some fruit off our branches or that He might make our light burn more brightly. He is the One who pours in the oil, which represents the Holy Spirit. I get so tired today of hearing people say, "The Holy Ghost this, and the Holy Ghost that." My friend, Jesus Christ is the Head of the church. He is the One who sent the Holy Spirit into the world. He said that when the Holy Spirit came He would do certain things, not just any old thing you want Him to do. The Holy Spirit is doing what the Lord Jesus sent Him into the world to do. Christ is the Head of the church. The Lord wants light, and He is the One who pours in the Holy Spirit to get that light. If there is any light coming from my ministry, it comes from the Holy Spirit. He is the source. No light originates in Vernon McGee. I found that out a long time ago.

Christ does something else, and it makes me shiver. He sometimes uses a snuffer. If a lamp won't give good light and it keeps smoking up the place, the Lord Jesus snuffs it out. This is what John meant when he said that there is a sin unto death (see 1 John 5:16). You and I can be set aside. Oh, the number of people whom I have known to be set aside—preachers and elders and deacons and Sunday school teachers! Christ put them aside. He is walking in the midst of the lampstands, and He wants them to produce light.

> His head and his hairs were white like wool, as white as snow; and his eyes were as a flame of fire;
>
> And his feet like unto fine brass, as if they burned in a furnace; and his voice as the sound of many waters [Rev. 1:14–15].

"His head and his hairs were white like wool, as white as snow" speaks of His eternal existence. He is the Ancient of Days (see Dan. 7:9).

"His eyes were as a flame of fire" speaks of His penetrating insight and eyewitness knowledge of the total life of the church. He knows all about you. He knows all about me. He sat over the treasury and watched how the people gave. Last Sunday He watched you when you put your offering in the plate. You didn't think anybody knew what you gave, did you? Also, His eyes met those of Simon Peter after he had denied Him. After that happened, Peter went out and wept. If you could only see the eyes of your Savior today! My friend, He is looking at us.

"His feet like unto fine brass" or burnished brass is symbolic of judgment. That brass or brazen altar outside the tabernacle proper represents Christ's work down here on earth when He died on the cross. It was there that He bore your judgment and my judgment for sin. And now He is judging those of us who are His own.

General Nathan Twining was the man who gave the command to drop the first atom bombs on Hiroshima and Nagasaki. He later became the chairman of the U.S. Joint Chiefs of Staff, and he dropped another "atom bomb" on December 10, 1959, and it had just about as great a repercussion as the literal bomb did. He dropped the latter bomb when he told the French in particular, and the other European countries in general, that they were not carrying their share of the defense of NATO and that they were falling down on their responsibility in defending Europe. He told them that NATO was coming unglued. The repercussions from his announcement are still reverberating through Europe today. Although General Twining was accurate in his charges, the reaction was bitter, and there were counter charges made, and denials and excuses were offered. About that time, when President Eisenhower went to Europe, he received the coolest reception he had ever experienced. Why? The human heart resents criticism.

Human nature rebels against judgment being passed upon it. Man likes to be handed a passel of little rules and regulations which he can keep. That is the reason so many study courses are popular with Christians—they want to be legalistic. They don't want to live by grace. Give Christians a few little rules they can go by, and they are very happy. The result, however, is a group of Band-Aid believers. They put on a little Band-Aid here and another one there, and they think that is all that is necessary to heal a broken leg. Why? The human nature that man has will purr like a pussycat when flattered, but it will bristle like a porcupine when failure to do a job is noted. That is the reason that the present position of Christ and His contemporary work of inspection are largely ignored by the church. He occupies the position of Judge of the church, and He does not flatter; He does not ignore what He sees; He does not shut His eyes to sin and wrongdoing. His constant charge and command to His own is "Repent!" We are going to see this as we move along in the Book of Revelation. He says to His church, "Change or I will come to you and I will remove your lampstand" (see Rev. 2:5). The church has smarted and squirmed under this indictment down through the ages and still does. This is the result of the natural resentment that is in the hearts of lukewarm believers. And the "Laodicean" church pays scant attention to what Christ has to say. As someone has said, "There is a Man in glory, but the church has lost sight of Him."

"His voice as the sound of many waters" is the voice of authority—the voice that called this universe into existence, the voice that will raise His own from the grave, the voice that will take His own out of the world to be with Him.

All these figures add to the picture of Christ as our Great High Priest, inspecting and judging His church. Consider your Great High Priest. The Spirit of God will help you see Him in all of His beauty and glory. How wonderful He is!

> **And he had in his right hand seven stars: and out of his mouth went a sharp two-edged sword: and his countenance was as the sun shineth in his strength [Rev. 1:16].**

"He had in his right hand seven stars" means that He controls this universe.

"Out of his mouth went a sharp two-edged sword." One man asked me, "Do you think that a literal sword goes out of His mouth?" Of course not! Scripture tells us that the sword represents His Word. In Hebrews 4:12 we read, "For the word of God is quick, and powerful, and sharper than any two-edged sword, piercing even to the dividing asunder of soul and spirit, and of the joints and marrow, and is a discerner of the thoughts and intents of the heart." God judges by His Word. He judges by it today. When He speaks the Word, my friend, you had better sit up and take note because He means business.

"His countenance was as the sun shineth in his strength." You can't even look at the sun. Do you think you will be able to look at the Creator who made the sun, the One who is the glorified Christ? How wonderful He is!

> **And when I saw him, I fell at his feet as dead. And he laid his right hand upon me, saying unto me, Fear not; I am the first and the last [Rev. 1:17].**

John is the disciple who had an easy familiarity with Christ on earth. He is the man who reclined upon His bosom in the Upper Room. John was very close to the Lord Jesus—in fact, he didn't mind rebuking Him on an occasion. But when he saw the glorified Christ on the Isle of Patmos, he did not go up to Him and pat Him on the back or shake hands with Him. He didn't even try to begin a conversation. He fell at His feet as dead! The effect of the vision upon John was nothing short of paralyzing.

My friend, since John reacted like that, we can be sure that when you and I get into the presence of the Lord Jesus, we are not going to approach Him in a familiar way. We will fall at His feet as dead. He is the glorified Christ today. And let me say that I do not like the irreverence of the "Jesus culture" that we see today, speaking of Him or to Him as if He were a buddy. Nor do I like to hear someone sing or say that Jesus is a friend of theirs. Now, you may think I am hard to please. You are right; I am. But Jesus said, "Ye are my friends, if ye do whatsoever I command you" (John 15:14). If you say that Jesus is a friend of yours, you must be implying that you are obeying Him. Oh, my friend, if we could see Him in all of His glory and His beauty, we would not get familiar with Him.

But the marvelous thing is that He says, "Fear not." This is the greeting of Deity addressing humanity. And He gives four reasons why we should not fear.

1. "I am the first and the last." This speaks of His deity. He came out of eternity, and He moves into eternity. The psalmist says, "Before the mountains were brought forth, or ever thou hadst formed the earth and the world, even from everlasting to everlasting, thou art God" (Ps. 90:2). The word *everlasting* means from the vanishing point in the past to the vanishing point in the future He is God. He is first because there were none before Him, and He is last for there are none to follow Him.

I am he that liveth, and was dead; and, behold, I am alive for evermore, Amen; and have the keys of hell and of death [Rev. 1:18].

2. "I am he that liveth, and was dead"—or, the living One who became dead. This speaks of His redemptive death and resurrection. Most of us have a guilt complex. We are afraid somebody will point a finger at us and say, "You are guilty." We are, of course, but Paul deals with this question in Romans 8:34, where he says, "Who is he that condemneth? It is Christ that died, yea rather, that is risen again, who is even at the right hand of God, who also maketh intercession for us."

Where is the fellow who is going to condemn you? Paul says, "Who is he that condemneth? It is Christ who died." Do you find fault with me? Do you say I am a great sinner? I want you to know that Christ died for me, and He is risen from the dead. He rose for my justification to show that I am forgiven and that I am going to heaven someday. And He is even at the right hand of God—how wonderful—and He makes intercession, that is, He prays for me. We see this in His next reason:

3. "And, behold, I am alive for evermore." This refers to His present state. He is not only judging, but He is also making intercession for us. How we need that!

4. "And have the keys of death and of hades." The keys speak of authority and power. Jesus has power over death and the grave right now—because of His own death and resurrection. *Hades* is the Greek word for the unseen world. It can refer to the grave where the body is laid or to the place where the spirit goes.

My friend, you and I can take comfort in the fact that Jesus has the keys of death. He is the One who can relieve us of the terrible fear of death.

TIME DIVISION OF THE APOCALYPSE'S CONTENTS

The following verses give us the chronological order and division of this Book of Revelation in three time series: past, present, and future. Right now I am making this division arbitrarily, and then as we progress through the book I can demonstrate that it is accurate.

Write the things which thou hast seen, and the things which are, and the things which shall be hereafter [Rev. 1:19].

1. "Write the things which thou hast seen." Up to this point what had John seen? He had seen the glorified Christ. Let me remind you that this is a Christocentric book. The glorified Christ is the subject. Don't get your eyes on the horsemen or on the bowls of wrath or on the beasts—they are just passing through. Fix your eyes on the Lord Jesus

Christ. He is the One who *was*, who is, and who *will* be. He is the same yesterday, today, and forever. And John is to write the vision he has had of Him.

2. "The things which are." What are the things that *are?* They are the things that pertain to the church, church things. And we are still here after nineteen hundred years. The matters concerning the church are recorded in chapters 2—3.

3. "The things which shall be hereafter." Or, as my own translation reads: *the things which you are about to see after these things* [*meta tauta*]. This is the program of Jesus Christ, and we shall see that the church goes to heaven, and then we shall see the things that take place on the earth after the church leaves it. This program of Christ is covered by chapters 4—22.

INTERPRETATION OF SEVEN STARS
AND SEVEN LAMPSTANDS

The mystery of the seven stars which thou sawest in my right hand, and the seven golden candlesticks. The seven stars are the angels of the seven churches: and the seven candlesticks which thou sawest are the seven churches [Rev. 1:20].

You see, John will make it clear when he is using symbols, and he will help us understand what the symbols mean. Otherwise, he is not using symbolic language but is talking about *literal* things.

"The mystery of the seven stars . . . and the seven . . . candlesticks." A mystery in Scripture means a sacred secret, that which has not been revealed before. And this had not been revealed before it was given to John. It pertains specifically to that which John has seen. He is the only one who has looked upon the glorified Christ. You may ask, "Hadn't Paul seen the glorified Christ?" Well, what did Paul see? He said that he saw ". . . a light from heaven, above the brightness of the sun . . ." (Acts 26:13). I can't even look at the sun, and I don't think Paul could have seen Christ in all of His glory, but he knew that He was there. The brightness even blinded Paul for a few days. Therefore, John was the first to see the glorified Christ.

The "seven stars" are identified as the "seven angels." The stars represent authority. In Jude, verse 13, apostates are called wandering stars. The word *angel* literally means "messenger" and may be either human or angelic beings. It could refer to a messenger of the angelic hosts of heaven or to a ruler or a teacher of a congregation on earth. I like to think that it refers to the local pastors of the seven churches which we are going to look at in the next two chapters. I like to hear a pastor called an angel because sometimes they are called other things. So, if you don't mind, I'll hold to that interpretation.

"The seven candlesticks which thou sawest are the seven churches." The English word *candlestick* should be *lampstand* since it holds lamps rather than candles. It represents the seven churches of Asia, as we shall see. Then, in turn, these represent the church as a whole, the church as the body of Christ.

INTRODUCTION TO
CHAPTERS 2 AND 3

This brings us to the section on the "church," which is also called the body of Christ. He loved the church and gave Himself for it. The church is the body of believers which the Father has given Him and for whom He prayed in John 17.

After chapter 3, the church is conspicuous by its absence. Up to chapter 4, the church is mentioned nineteen times. From chapter 4 through chapter 20 (the Great White Throne Judgment), the church is not mentioned one time. The normal reaction is to inquire as to the destination and location of the church during this period. It certainly is not in the world. It has been removed from the earth.

These seven letters have a threefold interpretation and application:

1. Contemporary—they had a direct message to the local churches of John's day. I intend to take you to the location of these seven churches in these next two chapters. I have visited the sites of these churches several times, and I want to visit them again and again, because it is such a thrill and because it brings me closer to the Bible. You can get closer to the Bible by visiting these seven churches than you can by walking through the land of Israel. The ruins have an obvious message. John was writing to churches that he knew all about. In *The Letters to the Seven Churches of Asia* Sir William Ramsay said, "The man who wrote these seven letters to the seven churches had been there, and he knew the local conditions."

2. Composite—each one is a composite picture of the church. There is something that is applicable to all churches in all ages in each message to each individual church. In other words, when you read the message to the church in Pergamum, there is a message for your church and a message for you personally.

3. Chronological—the panoramic history of the church is given in these seven letters, from Pentecost to the *Parousia*, from the Upper Room to the upper air. There are seven distinct periods of church history. Ephesus represents the apostolic church; Laodicea represents the

apostate church. This prophetic picture is largely fulfilled and is now church history, which makes these chapters extremely remarkable.

Now let me call your attention to the well-defined and definite format which the Lord Jesus used in each one of the letters to the seven churches.

1. There was some feature of the glorified Christ (whom John saw in chapter 1) that was emphasized in addressing each church. A particular thing was emphasized for a particular purpose, of course.

2. The letters are addressed to the angel of each church. As I have said, it is my understanding that the angel is just a human messenger whom we would designate as the pastor of the church.

3. He begins by stating to each, "I know thy works," although there has been some question about that in regard to a couple of the letters.

4. He first gives a word of commendation, and then He gives a word of condemnation. That is His method, but the exceptions should be noted. There is no word of condemnation to Smyrna or Philadelphia. Smyrna was the martyr church, and He is not about to condemn that church. Philadelphia was the missionary church that was getting out His Word, and He didn't condemn it. He has no word of commendation for Laodicea, the apostate church.

5. Each letter concludes with the warning, "He that hath an ear, let him hear what the Spirit saith."

In this second major division of the book, we see the things that are, that is, church-related things. Each of the seven letters is a message which the Lord Jesus sent to a particular church.

We today may not be conversant with the fact that in the first and second centuries letter-writing and travel were commonplace in the Roman Empire. There was extensive communication throughout the Roman Empire during that period. Therefore, the seven letters of the Apocalypse are very remarkable for other reasons, the most important of which is that they are direct letters from Christ to the churches. (This means that we have two epistles to the Ephesians—one that Paul wrote and one that the Lord Jesus gave through John.) Dr. Deissmann, in his book, *Light from the Ancient East*, made a distinction between letters and epistles which has been proven to be artifi-

cial and entirely false. The fact that these are called *letters* to the seven
churches rather than *epistles* does not lessen their importance. They
had an extensive outlet, and they reached multitudes of people. There
were many outstanding churches in the Roman Empire, but these
seven outstanding churches were chosen for several reasons, one of
which was that they were located in probably the most important area
of the Roman Empire during the first, second, and even third centuries. The area was important because it was where East and West met.
By 2000 B.C. there was a civilization along the coast of Asia Minor (the
modern west coast of Turkey). It is a very beautiful area. It reminds me
of Southern California—but without smog, of course. Not only is it
beautiful, but some of the richest land is there. In ancient times the
heart of the great Hittite nation was located there. Ephesus was
founded about 2000 B.C. by the Hittites, as was Smyrna (modern Izmir). Pergamum obviously was founded later, and then Thyatira and
Sardis even later, and they were made great during the time of Alexander the Great. The Anatolian civilization met the Greek civilization
there. You can always tell the difference because the gods of the Anatolians (a more primitive people) were beasts, whereas the gods of the
Greeks were projections and enlargements of human beings.

Ephesus was a city of about two hundred thousand people. It was a
great city and had a huge outdoor theater which could seat about
twenty thousand people. It was a place of resorts, and the Roman emperors came there. It was a city constructed of white marble, a beautiful place, and Paul commented on that. If we think that the impact of
the gospel was not great in that area, we are entirely mistaken. Such
was the impact of the gospel on Ephesus that four great pillars or tow-
ers were placed at the entrance to the harbor, and upon them was the
emblem of the cross. One monument was dedicated to Matthew, one
to Mark, one to Luke, and one to John. Only one pillar stands there
today, but it still bears the symbol of the cross. And there are other
evidences of the tremendous impact of the gospel where pagan temples were later turned into churches.

After the ministry of Paul and John, there was a tremendous Christian population in that area. It seems that Paul had his greatest ministry in the city of Ephesus, and Luke writes, ". . . all they which dwelt

in Asia heard the word of the Lord Jesus, both Jews and Greeks" (Acts 19:10). Not all turned to Christ, but everyone heard. That was probably the greatest movement that has ever taken place in the history of the church.

CHAPTER 2

THEME: The church in the world

Ephesus was not only a beautiful city, it was also the chief city of the province of Asia. It was called "the Vanity Fair of Asia." Pliny called it "the Light of Asia." It was both the religious and commercial center of that entire area which influenced both East and West—Asia and Europe. When Paul landed at the harbor in Ephesus, he looked down Harbor Boulevard, all in white marble. As he moved toward the center of the city, he saw all sorts of lovely buildings, temples, and gift shops. There was a large market on his right as he went up the boulevard, and ahead of him on the side of a mountain was a theater that seated twenty thousand people. Off to his left was the great amphitheater that seated over one hundred thousand people. At times there were as many as one to two million people gathered in Ephesus. It was here that Paul had his greatest ministry, and it was here that John later became pastor.

This city was first formed around the temple of Diana by the Anatolians who worshiped Diana. The first temple was a wooden structure, built in a low place very near the ocean—in fact, the waters lapped at the very base. In time, the Cayster and the little Maeander River brought down so much silt that, by the time of Alexander the Great, it had filled in around the temple. I have never seen any country that washes as much as that valley washes. The river itself is as thick as soup because it is carrying so much soil deposit. When Alexander took the city (by the way, the temple burned on the night Alexander was born), he turned it over to one of his generals, Lysimachus. Because the silt was coming and the harbor was filling up, Lysimachus moved the people to a higher location, and that is where the ruins of the city can be seen today. It is the city which was there when Paul came.

At the site of the old temple, a foundation of charcoal and skins was laid over this low, marshy place, and Alexander the Great led in the construction of a new temple of Diana which became one of the wonders of the ancient world. It was the largest Greek temple ever constructed. In it were over one hundred external columns about fifty-six feet in height, of which thirty-six were hand carved. The doors were of cypress wood; columns and walls were of Parian marble; the staircase was carved out of one vine from Cyprus.

The temple served as the bank of Asia and was the depository of vast sums of money. It was an art gallery displaying the masterpieces of Praxiteles, Phidias, Scopas, and Polycletus. Apelles' famous painting of Alexander was there. Behind a purple curtain was the lewd and crude image of Diana, the goddess of fertility. She was many-breasted, carried a club in one hand and a trident in the other. *Horrible* is Diana of the Ephesians could be accurately substituted for "Great is Diana of the Ephesians." Diana was the most sacred idol of heathenism. Her temple was four times larger than the Parthenon at Athens, and it was finally destroyed by the Goths in A.D. 256. Of course, it was standing in Paul's day. If you want to see something of the magnificence of the place, go to Istanbul, to the Hagia Sophia. Those beautiful green columns that are there were taken out of the temple of Diana by Justinian when he built Hagia Sophia. Seeing only these columns gives us some conception of the beauty of the temple of Diana.

Around the temple of Diana were performed the grossest forms of immorality. She was worshiped by probably more people than was any other idol. The worshipers indulged in the basest religious rites of sensuality and the wildest bacchanalian orgies that were excessive and vicious. And farther inland, the worship of Diana became nothing more than sex orgies, and her name was changed from Diana to Cybele.

Paul came to Ephesus on his third missionary journey to begin a ministry. For two years the Word of God went out from the school of Tyrannus. Of this experience Paul wrote, "For a great door and effectual is opened unto me, and there are many adversaries" (1 Cor. 16:9). Later John, the "apostle of love" and the "son of thunder," came to Ephesus as a pastor. He was exiled to Patmos, then after about ten years of being exiled and imprisoned, he returned to Ephesus. The

Basilica of Saint John, which is located on the highest point there, is built over the traditional burial spot of the apostle John.

CHRIST'S LETTER TO THE CHURCH IN EPHESUS

The Lord Jesus Christ speaks to this church in the midst of crass materialism, degraded animalism, base paganism, and dark heathenism. Note this carefully, because I consider this message to be one of the most important of all.

> Unto the angel of the church of Ephesus write; These things saith he that holdeth the seven stars in his right hand, who walketh in the midst of the seven golden candlesticks [Rev. 2:1].

This is my translation:

> Unto the messenger of the church in Ephesus write; These things saith the One holding the seven stars in His right hand, the One walking (up and down) in the midst of the seven golden lampstands.

Notice that He holds in His hand the church. It is under His control. He doesn't have that control now, but He did then. "He walketh" literally means that He is walking up and down. I believe that He is still walking up and down in our day and that He is still judging the church.

He has seven words of commendation for this church:

> I know thy works, and thy labour, and thy patience, and how thou canst not bear them which are evil: and thou hast tried them which say they are apostles, and are not, and hast found them liars:

> And hast borne, and hast patience, and for my name's sake hast laboured, and hast not fainted [Rev. 2:2–3].

1. "I know thy works." We need to understand that He is speaking to believers. The Lord Jesus does not ask the lost world for good works. For example, "Not by works of righteousness which we have done, but according to his mercy he saved us, by the washing of regeneration, and renewing of the Holy Ghost" (Titus 3:5). In Romans 4:5 Paul says, "But to him that worketh not, but believeth on him that justifieth the ungodly, his faith is counted for righteousness." Christ is talking to His own. After you are saved, He wants to talk to you about good works. He has a lot to say about this subject. In Ephesians 2:8–10 we read, "For by grace are ye saved through faith; and that not of yourselves: it is the gift of God: not of works, lest any man should boast. For we are his workmanship, created in Christ Jesus unto good works, which God hath before ordained that we should walk in them." Paul could write to Titus, "They profess that they know God; but in works they deny him, being abominable, and disobedient, and unto every good work reprobate" (Titus 1:16). Someone has said, "The Christian ought to be like a good watch—all gold, open-faced, well-regulated, dependable, and filled with good works." The Lord Jesus is saying to the church in Ephesus, as Paul had said, ". . . be filled with the [Holy] Spirit" (Eph. 5:18). And Paul went on to tell them what they could do as Spirit-filled believers. And now the Lord Jesus commends them for their good works.

2. "I know . . . thy labour." What is the difference between work and labor? The word *labor* carries a meaning of weariness. In the Gospel record it says that Jesus became wearied with His journey. That was the weariness which Ephesian believers experienced. They suffered weariness in their labor for Him.

3. "I know . . . thy patience." Patience is a fruit of the Holy Spirit.

4. "How thou canst not bear them which are evil." They would not endure evil men.

5. "Thou hast tried them which say they are apostles, and are not, and hast found them liars." They tested everyone who came to Ephesus claiming to be an apostle. They would ask them if they had seen the resurrected Christ, and they soon found out whether or not they were really apostles. If they were not, they asked them to leave town.

The Lord Jesus commended them for testing men, and I feel this is more needed today than it was even then.

6. "Hast borne . . . for my name's sake hast laboured." For His name's sake they were bearing the Cross. They preached Christ. They believed in the virgin birth of Christ; they believed in His deity; they believed in His sacrificial death and resurrection. And they paid a price for their belief.

7. "And hast not fainted." More accurately, it is "hast not grown weary." What does He mean by this? Earlier He said that they had grown weary, and now He says they have not grown weary. Well, this is one of the great paradoxes of the Christian faith. I can illustrate it by what Dwight L. Moody once said when he came home exhausted after a campaign and his family begged him not to go to the next campaign. He said to them, "I grow weary *in* the work but not *of* the work." There is a lot of difference. You can get weary *in* the work of Christ, but it is tragic if you get weary *of* the work of Christ.

These seven words of commendation, which the Lord Jesus gave to the local church at Ephesus, also apply to the period of church history between Pentecost and A.D. 100, which the Ephesian church represents.

Now He has one word of condemnation:

Nevertheless I have somewhat against thee, because thou hast left thy first love [Rev. 2:4].

Nevertheless I have against thee that thou art leaving thy best love.

They had lost that intense and enthusiastic devotion to the person of Christ. It is difficult for us to sense the state to which the Holy Spirit had brought this church. He had brought the believers in Ephesus into an intimate and personal relationship to Jesus Christ. He had brought them to the place where they could say to the Lord, "We *love* you." This may seem like a very unimportant thing to us today, but their love for the Lord was very important to Christ. He was saying to the

Ephesians, "You are leaving your best love." They hadn't quite departed from that love, but they were on the way. It is difficult for us in this cold, skeptical, cynical, and indifferent day in which we live to understand this. The world has intruded into the church to such an extent that it is hard for us to conceive of the intense, enthusiastic devotion the early church gave to the person of Christ. The early church first went off the track not in their doctrine but in their personal relationship to Jesus Christ.

Ephesus was a great city, and it had many attractions that were beginning to draw believers away from their first love for Jesus Christ. This was the church that became so potent in its evangelism in that area of about twenty-five million people that even the Roman emperors and the nobility of that day had an opportunity to hear the gospel. In that area there was such a mighty moving of the Spirit of God that it has probably never been duplicated since.

Every now and then we meet someone or read about someone who has had that close personal relationship with Christ. David Brainard, the missionary to Indians in this country, was such a man. He suffered from what was then called consumption (we know it as tuberculosis). He would travel to the Indians by horseback, and sometimes he would have a convulsion, vomit blood, become unconscious, and fall off his horse. He would lie in the snow, and when that happened, his horse learned to stay right there. When he regained consciousness, he would crawl back onto his horse and be on his way to preach to the Indians. As he went, he would cry out, "Lord Jesus, I've failed You, but You know that I love You." He had that close, intimate relationship with Christ.

My friend, that personal relationship is all-important in our day, also. We are so involved in methods—I am rather amused at some of the Band-Aid courses which are being offered—and they are making Band-Aid believers. Generally, the course is some little legal system that gives you certain rules to follow and certain psychological patterns to observe which will enable you to solve all your problems. They try to teach you how to get along with yourself (that's a pretty big order!), with your neighbors, and especially with your wife. All of

those relationships are very important, and a great many people think
that if they can follow a few rules, they will have the key to a successful Christian life. My friend, let me put it in a nutshell by asking one
question: Do you love Jesus Christ? I don't care what your system is,
what your denomination is, what your program is, what little set of
rules you follow, they will all come to naught if you don't love Him.
Although some systems are better than others, almost any system
will work if you love Christ. An intimate relationship with Christ will
make all of your relationships and all of your Christian service a joy.

The story is told in New England about two girls who worked in a
cotton mill. They were friends, but when one of them quit working
there, they lost touch with each other. Finally, they met one day on the
street. The working girl asked her friend.

"Are you still working?"

"No," she said, "I got married!"

When that girl worked in the mill, she watched the clock, and every
evening when five o'clock came, she had her coat on and was on her
way out. It was hard work, and she didn't like it. Now she is married
and she says that she has quit working.

Well, if you could look at her life, you wouldn't think she had quit
working. She gets up earlier than ever before to prepare breakfast for
her husband and to pack his lunch. Then she throws her arms around
him as she tells him good-bye. All day long she is busy cleaning
house and washing clothes and caring for two little brats who are two
little angels to her because they are hers. Then when five o'clock
comes, she doesn't put on her coat and leave; she starts cooking dinner. About six o'clock here comes her husband. She is right there at
the door to throw her arms around him and tell him how much she has
missed him that day. When a man comes home in the evening, opens
the door, and hears a voice from upstairs or from the rear of the house
calling, "Is that you?", he knows the honeymoon is over. But this girl
is in love. Her husband's workday is over, but hers has only just gotten
started. She serves dinner to her husband and feeds the children.
Then she washes the dishes, puts the children to bed—and that's not
easy—and works around getting things ready for her husband for the

next day. I tell you she is weary when she finally gets into bed—but she's not working anymore, she says! Why? Because she is in love. That's the difference.

My friend, when your home life and your church life become a burden, there is something wrong with your relationship with Christ. When you get that straightened out, other things will straighten out also.

This is the reason the Lord Jesus said to the Ephesian believers, "You are getting away from your first love, your best love." What is the solution for them?

> **Remember therefore from whence thou art fallen, and repent, and do the first works; or else I will come unto thee quickly, and will remove thy candlestick out of his place, except thou repent [Rev. 2:5].**

"Remember." That is the first thing they were to do. Memory is a marvelous thing. Someone has said that God has given us memories so we can have roses in December. Well, here in California we have short memories so we have roses all year-round. But memory is a wonderful thing. Someone else has said that memory is a luxury that only a good man can enjoy. My friend, do you remember when you were converted? Do you remember what a thrill it was and what the Lord Jesus meant to you? Have you become cold and indifferent to Him? Are you in a backslidden condition? Remember. Remember where you once were. You can get back to that same place.

"And repent." Believe me, Christians need to repent. We need to break the shell of self-sufficiency, the crust of conceit, the shield of sophistication, the veneer of vanity, get rid of the false face of "piosity," and stop this business of everlastingly polishing our halo as if we were some great saint. Repent! Repentance means to turn back to Him, and it is the message for believers. How dare the church tell an unsaved man to repent. What he needs to do is to turn to Christ for salvation. When he turns to Christ, he will turn from his sin—as the Thessalonians ". . . turned to God from idols to serve the living and true God; And to wait for his Son from heaven . . ." (1 Thess. 1:9–10).

But the church needs to repent, and that is the message they do not want to hear today. Remember, repent, and return unto Him.

"Or else I will come unto thee quickly, and will remove the candlestick out of his place, except thou repent." Christ says that He will remove your lampstand. Oh, how many churches in our day have been practically closed. Once the crowds came, but they don't come anymore because the Word of God is no longer being taught. My friend, Christ is still watching the lamps, and He doesn't mind trimming the wicks or even using the snuffer when they refuse to give light.

> **But this thou hast, that thou hatest the deeds of the Nicolaitans, which I also hate [Rev. 2:6].**

Nicolaitans is a compound word. *Nikao* means "to conquer," and *laos* means "the people." We get our word *laity* from that. It is difficult to identify who the Nicolaitans were. Some scholars think that they were a priestly order which was beginning to take shape and attempt to rule over the people. Another theory is that there is no way to identify this group in any of the early or late churches. The third explanation is that there was a man by the name of Nicolaus of Antioch, who apostatized from the truth and formed an Antinomian Gnostic cult which taught (among other doctrines) that one must indulge in sin in order to understand it. They gave themselves over to sensuality with the explanation that such sins did not touch the spirit. That "Nicolaitans" refers to this cult is probably the best explanation. The church in Ephesus hated it. A little later on we will see that the church in Pergamos [Pergamum] tolerated it.

> **He that hath an ear, let him hear what the Spirit saith unto the churches; To him that overcometh will I give to eat of the tree of life, which is in the midst of the paradise of God [Rev. 2:7].**

"He that hath an ear." This is what I call a "blood-tipped ear," which was the requirement for the Old Testament priests. Not everyone can hear the Word of God. Oh, I know they can hear the audible sound, but they miss the message. The Lord Jesus uses the phrase to alert dull ears. We learn from the Gospel records that He often used that expression. He said that they have ears to hear but they hear not. Now He speaks to those with spiritual perception.

"Let him hear what the Spirit saith unto the churches." "The Spirit" is the Holy Spirit, the Teacher of the church.

"To him that overcometh" refers to genuine believers, and we can overcome only through the blood of the Lamb.

"Will I give to eat of the tree of life." You will recall that man was forbidden to eat of the Tree of Life after the Fall, as recorded in Genesis 3:22–24. But in heaven the "no trespassing" sign will be taken down, and all of us will be given the privilege of eating of the Tree of Life. I don't know what kind of fruit it has, but I believe it will enable us really to live it up. Most of us don't know much about living yet. We have sort of a vegetable existence down here, but we will have a good fruit existence up there—we'll eat of the Tree of Life. We are going to live as we have never lived before.

"The paradise of God" means the garden of God. Heaven is a garden of green primarily and is not just a place with streets of gold.

The church of Ephesus represents the church at its best, the apostolic church.

CHRIST'S LETTER TO THE CHURCH IN SMYRNA

Smyrna is the martyr church, the church that suffered martyrdom for Christ. The word Smyrna means "myrrh" and carries the meaning of suffering.

The city of Smyrna is still in existence in our day. It has a Turkish name, Izmir, which may lead you astray, but it is the same city. It has been continuously inhabited from the time it was founded. I have been there; in fact, we stay in Izmir when we visit the sites of the early churches in that area. It is a commercial city. There are those who have told us that Izmir will soon be larger than Istanbul. It will certainly be a larger commercial center. There is a tremendous population there.

The modern city covers so much of the ruins of ancient Smyrna that you are apt to miss the beauty which was there.

I have taken some pictures of it and use them as slides in an illustrated message. I try to point out the beauty of that harbor. It is very large and one of the most beautiful harbors that I have seen. In fact, Smyrna was one of the loveliest cities of Asia. It was called a flower, an ornament, and it has been called the crown of all Asia. The acropolis is located on Mount Pagos. In fact, the early city that goes back to about 2000 B.C., a Hittite city at that time, was built around the slope of Mount Pagos. Later Alexander the Great had a great deal to do with building it into the beautiful city that it became. There were wide boulevards along the slopes of Mount Pagos. Smyrna was called the crown city because the acropolis was encircled with flowers, a hedge, and myrtle trees. The city was adorned with noble buildings and beautiful temples—a temple of Zeus, a temple of Cybele (Diana), a temple of Aphrodite, a temple of Apollo, and a temple of Asclepius. Smyrna had a theater and an odeum, that is, a music center—it was the home of music. Also it had a stadium, and it was at that stadium that Polycarp, bishop of Smyrna and student of the apostle John, was martyred, burned alive in A.D. 155.

In Christian literature, Smyrna means "suffering." The Lord Jesus, in His letter addressed to the church there, said that He knew their sufferings and their poverty. He had no word of condemnation for them or for the church at Philadelphia. They were the churches that heard no word of condemnation from Him, and it is interesting that these two cities, Smyrna and Philadelphia, are the only two which have had a continuous existence. Their lampstand has really been moved, but there are a few Christians in Izmir. Although they are under cover, they have made indirect contact with us when we have been there. They do not come out in the open because Christians are persecuted even today in modern Turkey.

As Ephesus represents the apostolic church, so Smyrna represents the martyr church which covers the period from about A.D. 100 to approximately A.D. 314, from the death of the apostle John to the Edict of Toleration by Constantine, which was given in A.D. 313 and ended the persecution of Christians—not only in Smyrna but all over the Roman Empire.

Now here we have the Lord Jesus addressing the church at Smyrna. It is His briefest message, and it is all commendatory—everything He has to say to them is praise.

> **And unto the angel of the church in Smyrna write; These things saith the first and the last, which was dead, and is alive [Rev. 2:8].**

> *And to the messenger of the church in Smyrna, write, These things saith the first and the last, who became dead, and lived.*

This verse is a reference to chapter 1, verses 17-18, which says, "And when I saw him, I fell at his feet as dead. And he laid his right hand upon me, saying unto me, Fear not; I am the first and the last: I am he that liveth, and was dead; and, behold, I am alive for evermore, Amen; and have the keys of hell and of death." The Lord chose from the vision of Himself that particular figure which was fitting for each church. To the church in Smyrna the Lord describes Himself as "the first and the last, which was dead, and is alive."

"The first and the last" means that there was nothing before Him and there will be nothing to follow Him. He has the final disposition of all things. The persecuted believers needed to know that He was the One in charge and that the persecution was in the planning and purpose of God.

"Who became dead, and lived" has a real message for martyrs. His experience with death identified Him with the five million who were martyred during this period. (According to *Fox's Book of Martyrs*, five million believers died for Christ during this period.) Christ was triumphant over death and can save to the uttermost those who are enduring persecution and martyrdom.

He has something further to say to them—

> **I know thy works, and tribulation, and poverty, (but thou art rich) and I know the blasphemy of them which**

say they are Jews, and are not, but are the synagogue of Satan.

Fear none of those things which thou shalt suffer: behold, the devil shall cast some of you into prison, that ye may be tried; and ye shall have tribulation ten days: be thou faithful unto death, and I will give thee a crown of life [Rev. 2:9–10].

There are seven things in this church which the Lord commended:

1. "Tribulation" is mentioned first. The word *works* is not in the best manuscripts. I prefer to leave it out, but if you want to include it, fine. Remember, this is not the Great Tribulation; it means simply trouble. Since the awful persecution of the church by the Roman emperors is not called the Great Tribulation, surely our small sufferings are not the Great Tribulation. But the church in Smyrna endured much tribulation, and they suffered for the Lord Jesus Christ.

2. "Poverty" denotes the lack of material possessions. The early church was made up largely of the poorer classes. When the wealthy believed in Christ, their property was confiscated because of their faith. "But thou art rich" denotes the spiritual wealth of the church—they were blessed with all spiritual blessings. Notice the contrast to the rich church in Laodicea. To that church He said, "You think you are rich, but you are really poor and don't know it."

When I am a visiting conference speaker in churches across the land, pastors like to tell me about the millionaire or persons of prominence whom they have in their congregation. Well, the martyr church couldn't brag about that. They had in their congregation slaves, ex-slaves, runaway slaves, freed slaves, poor people, and those who had lost whatever money they had when they became Christians.

3. "The blasphemy of them which say they are Jews . . . but are the synagogue of Satan." The implication is that the Jews in Smyrna who had come to Christ were Jews inwardly as well as outwardly. In Romans 9:6 Paul says that not all Israel is Israel. It is his religion that makes a Jew a real Jew. His religion is the thing that identifies him. Speaking of them nationally, the Lord said that their father was ". . . a Syrian ready to perish . . ." (Deut. 26:5). But Smyrna was a city of

culture in which many Jews had discarded their belief in the Old Testament. Although they said they were Jews, when a Jew gives up his religion, there is a question whether or not he is a Jew. In Germany many tried to do that, by the way. Down through the years there has been only a remnant of these people who have truly been God's people.

4. "Fear none of those things" is the encouragement of the Lord to His own in the midst of persecutions. This is the second time in this book that the Lord has offered this encouragement. History tells us that multitudes went to their death singing praises to God.

5. "The devil [Satan] shall cast some of you into prison." We are going to look at this fearful creature later on, but Christ labels him as being responsible for the suffering of the saints in Smyrna. You and I tend to blame the immediate person or circumstance which serves as Satan's tool, but the Lord Jesus goes back to the root trouble.

I would like to insert a personal word at this point. I could classify and pigeonhole everything that has come into my life as God's judgment or God's chastisement, but when I began experiencing so many physical problems, I was puzzled. Then quite a few people began writing to say, "I believe Satan is responsible for the things that are happening to you." And I decided this must be the explanation for the many physical problems that afflicted me.

6. "Ye shall have tribulation ten days." There were ten intense periods of persecution by ten Roman emperors (these dates are approximate):

    Nero—64–68 (Paul was beheaded under his reign)
    Domitian—95–96 (John was exiled during that period)
    Trajan—104–117 (Ignatius was burned at the stake)
    Marcus Aurelius—161–180 (Polycarp was martyred)
    Severus—200–211
    Maximinius—235–237
    Decius—250–253
    Valerian—257–260
    Aurelian—270–275
    Diocletian—303–313 (the worst emperor of all).

7. "Be thou faithful unto death"—and they were. They were martyrs for Him. He promises them "a crown of life." Remember that He is addressing the believers who lived in Smyrna, the crown city. It is interesting that to them He is saying that He will give crowns—not crowns of flowers—or of anything else perishable—but crowns that will be eternal.

The Lord has special crowns for those who suffer. I know many wonderful saints who are going to get that crown some day. My friend, if you are suffering at this moment and you have wondered if He cares, He has something good for you in eternity. You will get something that no one else will be getting, except others in your condition. God's Word says, "Blessed is the man that endureth temptation: for when he is tried, he shall receive the crown of life, which the Lord hath promised to them that love him" (James 1:12). That crown of life means that you are really going to live it up someday. What a glorious prospect that is for invalids and those on beds of pain today.

**He that hath an ear, let him hear what the Spirit saith
unto the churches; He that overcometh shall not be hurt
of the second death [Rev. 2:11].**

"He that hath an ear, let him hear what the Spirit saith unto the churches." Have you heard Him today? Is He speaking to you?

"The second death." Dwight L. Moody put it like this: "He who is born once will die twice; he who is born twice will die once." And if the Rapture occurs during his lifetime, he won't even have to die that one time. The "second death" is the death which no believer will experience. The first death concerns the body. The second death concerns the soul and the spirit; it is eternal separation from God. No believer will have to undergo that.

CHRIST'S LETTER TO THE CHURCH IN PERGAMUM

In our King James text this city is called Pergamos, but in Turkey it is called Pergamum, and I assume that is the correct spelling.

The church in Pergamum is representative of church history during the period of approximately A.D. 314 to A.D. 590. I call it *paganism unlimited* because during this time the world entered into the church and it began to move away from the person of Christ. This letter was Christ's message to the local church at Pergamum, of course, but it also has this historical significance.

First, let me give you the location of Pergamum. Izmir is the great city where tourists go because the airport and the hotels are there. You go about sixty-five miles south to reach Ephesus and about seventy miles north to reach Pergamum. These three were the royal cities, and they vied one with another. Smyrna (Izmir) was the great commercial center, Ephesus was the great political center, and Pergamum was the great religious center.

Pergamum was the capital of the kingdom of Pergamum. The acropolis still stands there, and the ruins of the great temples and the city are on top of it. It was a city in Mysia, labeled by Pliny "by far the most illustrious of Asia." It is one of the most beautiful spots in Asia Minor. Sir William Ramsay says that it was the one city that deserved to be called a royal city. In it was a temple built to Caesar Augustus, which made it a royal city. Augustus came to this beautiful area when the climate got cold in Rome. There was a healing spa there. It was not the commercial city that Smyrna was because it was not a seacoast town and it was off the great trade routes which came out of the Orient. But it was a fortified, stronghold city, built to withstand the enemy. It was built on a mountain, and the acropolis dominated the whole region of the broad plain of the Caicus. The original city was built between the two rivers which flowed into the Caicus and entirely surrounded this huge rocky hill, this promontory that stood out there alone. To visit it makes quite an impression. First you see that great mountain standing there, and you see the ruins on top.

Not only did Pergamum boast great temples, but it also had the greatest library of the pagan world. It was a library of over two hundred thousand volumes. In fact, the city got its name from the parchment (pergamena) which was used. This great library was the one which Marc Antony gave to his girl friend, Cleopatra. She lugged it off to Alexandria in Egypt, and that library was considered the greatest library the world has ever seen—and it originally came from Pergamum.

If you are ever in Istanbul and go into Hagia Sophia, you will see there a great alabaster vase, taller than I am and a thing of beauty, which was brought there from Pergamum. Of course, the city of Pergamum was rifled and denuded by the enemy when they finally took the city and destroyed it.

> And to the angel of the church in Pergamos write; These things saith he which hath the sharp sword with two edges [Rev. 2:12].

"To the angel of the church in Pergamos." This letter was addressed, as were other letters, to the angel or messenger of the church, which was probably the one we would call the pastor.

"These things saith he which hath the sharp sword with two edges" means the Word of God. The Word of God has the answer to man's need and man's sin, which in Pergamum was false religion. It was a city that emphasized religion, and the only way it could be reached would be by the Word of God.

> I know thy works and where thou dwellest, even where Satan's seat is: and thou holdest fast my name, and hast not denied my faith, even in those days wherein Antipas was my faithful martyr, who was slain among you, where Satan dwelleth [Rev. 2:13].

"Where thou dwellest." The Lord commends this church for three very definite things. First, He takes note of their circumstances. He knew that these believers were living in a very difficult place. And, my friend, the Lord takes note of our circumstances. Sometimes we are inclined to condemn someone who is caught in a certain set of circumstances, but if we were in the same position, we might act in an even worse way than he is acting.

"Even where Satan's seat [throne] is" reveals that religion was big business in Pergamum and that Satan's headquarters were there. This ought to settle the question for those who think that Satan is in hell at the present time. He has never yet been in hell because hell hasn't opened up for business yet. Satan will not be in hell until much later, as we shall see in chapter 20. At the present, Satan is loose and is the prince of this world, controlling kingdoms and going up and down the earth as a roaring lion, hunting for whom he may devour (see 1 Pet. 5:8). But he does have headquarters, and Christ said they were in Pergamum at that time. Since those days, I think that he has moved his headquarters around to different places. I used to get the impression that he had moved them to Los Angeles, and he may have done so because that is another great religious center of every kind of cult and "ism" and schism.

The reason our Lord said that Satan's throne was in Pergamum was because of the heathen temples there. Of course, all of this is in ruins today. There are markers and some reconstruction going on there now. But in John's day it was Satan's throne. As you enter the gate of the city, you see that the first temple to your right is the imposing temple of Athena. Directly above it is the great library. You would see the great temple of Caesar Augustus and Hadrian's great temple, which covers quite a bit of territory. There are other things that are quite interesting. There is the great altar to Zeus with an idol on it near the palace of the king. It is a very impressive spot, and some folk believe that it was the throne of Satan. Well, I think that it is included but that Satan's throne is a combination of all of these.

There are two other areas which are especially outstanding. One of them is the temple of Dionysius. I crawled down the side of that mountain to get pictures of the ruins of the temple of Dionysius, which is beside the ruins of the theater there. Some folk asked me why I did that. Well, Dionysius is the same as Bacchus, the god of wine, the goat-god. He is depicted with horns, but with his upper part as a man and his lower part as a goat, with cloven feet and a tail. In our day that is the modern idea of Satan, but the notion that Satan has horns, cloven feet, and a forked tail did not come from the Bible. Where did it come from? Well, it came from the temple of Dionysius, the god Bacchus, the god of wine or alcohol. My friend, we ought to be proud that we are Americans, but we also need to bow our heads in shame. Do you know how we got this country in which we live? We got it from the Indians (and I guess they got it from someone else), but the way we got it was not by bullets but by alcohol. Also Hawaii was taken away from the Hawaiians by giving them liquor. Alcohol has taken more territory than anything else. Satan is the god of liquor all right!

Then the other outstanding temple was of the god Asklepios. Down from that great promontory was the greatest hospital of the ancient world. It was the Mayo Clinic of that day. It was, first of all, a *temple* to Asklepios. If you are looking at the Greek god Asklepios, it is a man, but when you see the Anatolian or Oriental Asklepios, it is a serpent. There in Pergamum it was a serpent. I have pictures which I took of that great marble pillar which stands like an obelisk now but apparently was a pillar in the temple of Asklepios. The construction of the temple was unusual in that it was round. There they used every means of healing imaginable. They used both medicine and psychology—and about everything else.

Put yourself in this situation: you go down long tunnels, and above are holes that look like airholes for ventilation but are not. As you walk along these tunnels, sexy voices come down through the holes, saying to you, "You are going to get well. You are going to feel better. You are going to be healed." (Does that have a modern ring?) You go down to the hot baths where you are given a massage. There is a little theater there where they give plays of healing. If they haven't healed you by now, as a last resort they put you in that temple at night and turn loose the nonpoisonous snakes which crawl over you. (That is known as the shock treatment in our day!) If they don't heal you, they will drive you crazy, that's for sure. They have a back door where they take out the dead. They don't mention the ones they don't heal; they speak only of those who recover.

Caesar Augustus loved to go there. He wasn't exactly sick; he was an alcoholic. They just dried him out every year when he would come over. This was a great place, and for seven hundred years it was a hospital that people came to from all over the world. May I say to you, healing was *satanic* in those days. There is no question about the fact that there were good men there who used medicine, but basically, it was satanic. It was where Satan's throne was. That is important to see.

Now here is another word of commendation to the believers at Pergamum, "thou holdest fast my name." They were faithful in their defense of the deity of Christ.

As we have noted, the church at Pergamum is representative of the church in general during the years of A.D. 314 to approximately A.D. 590. Actually, it was an age that produced great giants of the faith. When the Arian heresy (which denied the deity of Christ) arose, Athanasius from North Africa was the great defender of the faith, and because of him the Council of Nicea in A.D. 325 condemned Arianism. And another man was Augustine, who answered the Pelagian heresy which denied original sin and the total corruption of human nature and also denied irresistible grace. These are two giants during this period who stood unshakably for the great doctrines of the faith.

"And hast not denied my faith" refers to the body of true doctrine which is believed by Christians.

"Even in those days wherein Antipas was my faithful martyr." Antipas was a martyr about whom we know nothing at all. He apparently was the first one at Pergamum, and there was a great company of martyrs who followed him.

So far Christ has had only words of commendation for the church at Pergamum, but now He condemns two things which were in that church—

> But I have a few things against thee, because thou hast there them that hold the doctrine of Balaam, who taught Balac to cast a stumblingblock before the children of Israel, to eat things sacrificed unto idols, and to commit fornication.
>
> So hast thou also them that hold the doctrine of the Nicolaitans, which thing I hate [Rev. 2:14–15].

The two items for condemnation were the doctrine of Balaam and the doctrine of the Nicolaitans. "The *doctrine* of Balaam" is different from the error of Balaam (see Jude 11), which revealed that Balaam thought that God would curse Israel because they were sinners. It is also different from the *way* of Balaam (see 2 Pet. 2:15), which was covetousness. But here in the verse before us, it is the *doctrine* or teaching of Balaam. He taught Balac the way to corrupt Israel by intermarriage with the Moabite women. This introduced into the nation of Israel both idolatry and fornication. And during the historical period which the church at Pergamum represents, the unconverted world came into the church.

"The doctrine of the Nicolaitans." We have seen that the church in Ephesus hated it, but here in Pergamum there were some who were holding that doctrine. Although we do not know exactly what the doctrine was, it probably was a gnostic cult developed by Nicolaus which advocated license in matters of Christians' conduct and apparently a return to religious rituals by clergy, ignoring the priesthood of all believers. Christ says that He *hates* it! You see, Christ hates as well as loves. We had better be careful that we are not indulging in the things that He hates.

> **Repent; or else I will come unto thee quickly, and will fight against them with the sword of my mouth [Rev. 2:16].**

"Repent." In other words, the only cure was repentance (*metanoēson*, "a change of mind"). God's Word says, "If we confess our sins, he is faithful and just to forgive us our sins, and to cleanse us from all unrighteousness" (1 John 1:9). If they would not repent, the Lord said He would fight against them with the sword of His mouth, which is the Word of God. What a mistake we make if we think that the church has the authority to decide what is right and what is wrong. The true church is made up of believers in Jesus Christ, and they form what Scripture calls the body of Christ. They are to be lights in the world. And if we are going to be lights in this dark world, we need to be careful to identify with the person of Jesus Christ and to recognize, not the church, but the Word of God as our authority.

**He that hath an ear, let him hear what the Spirit saith
unto the churches; To him that overcometh will I give to
eat of the hidden manna, and will give him a white
stone, and in the stone a new name written, which no
man knoweth saving he that receiveth it [Rev. 2:17].**

"He that hath an ear, let him hear what the Spirit saith unto the
churches." This is to you and me today.

"To him that overcometh" is the definition of a genuine Christian.
We overcome by the blood of the Lamb. Never are *we* overcomers, but
we overcome by His shed blood. We know that the victory was won by
Christ and not by ourselves.

"Hidden manna" speaks of the person and the death of Christ as
He is revealed in the Word of God. In fact, Jesus said that He Himself
was the Bread: "Then Jesus said unto them, Verily, verily, I say unto
you, Moses gave you not that bread from heaven; but my Father giveth
you the true bread from heaven. For the bread of God is he which
cometh down from heaven, and giveth life unto the world. Then said
they unto him, Lord, evermore give us this bread. And Jesus said unto
them, I am the bread of life: he that cometh to me shall never hunger;
and he that believeth on me shall never thirst" (John 6:32–35). The
believer needs to feed on Christ—this is a *must* for spiritual growth.
And, actually, Christ is hidden from view; He is not known or understood in our day. My, how folk misrepresent Him and abuse Him!

"I . . . will give him a white stone, and in the stone a new name
written, which no man knoweth saving he that receiveth it." A *white*
stone suggests that believers are not blackballed in heaven. Trench
said, "White is everywhere the color and livery of heaven." Frankly,
this is rather a difficult figure to interpret. But it is helpful to learn that
the people of Asia Minor to whom John was writing had a custom of
giving to intimate friends a *tessera*, a cube or rectangular block of
stone or ivory, with words or symbols engraved on it. It was a secret,
private possession of the one who received it. Well, Christ says that He
is going to give to each of His own a stone with a new name engraved
upon it. I do not believe that it will be a new name for you and me but
that it will be a new name for *Him*. I believe that each name will be

different because He means something different to each one of us. It will be His personal and intimate name to each of us.

CHRIST'S LETTER TO THE CHURCH IN THYATIRA

The church at Thyatira is representative of Romanism, which takes us into the Dark Ages from A.D. 590 to approximately A.D. 1000. It was a dark period.

When you leave Pergamum, you begin to move inland. Thyatira and the remaining three churches are inland. Thyatira was situated in a very beautiful location. Sir William Ramsay has written this about it:

> Thyatira was situated in the mouth of a long vale which extends north and south connecting the Hermus and Caicos Valleys. Down the vale a stream flows south to join the Lycus (near whose left bank Thyatira was situated), one of the chief tributaries of the Hermus, while its northern end is divided by only a ridge of small elevation from the Caicos Valley. The valleys of the two rivers, Hermus and Caicos, stretch east and west, opening down from the edge of the great central plateau of Anatolia towards the Ægean Sea. Nature has marked out this road, a very easy path, for the tide of communication which in all civilised times must have been large between the one valley and the other. The railway traverses its whole length now: in ancient times one of the chief routes of Asia Minor traversed it.

Thyatira was located in this long vale or pass. Thyatira was a city built for defense. However, most cities built for defense were situated upon an acropolis or a promontory and walls were put around them. But Thyatira was different. It stood in the middle of that vale on a very slight rising ground. Its strength lay in the fact that Rome stationed the elite guard there.

Thyatira was built by Lysimachus and again by Seleucus I, the founder of the Seleucid dynasty, whose vast realm extended from the Hermus Valley to the Himalayas. It finally fell to the enemy. No city in that area was so completely destroyed and rebuilt as was this city. For this reason, it is very disappointing to visit the ruins of Thyatira in our day. They cover only one very small block.

This city became prosperous under the sponsorship of Vespasian, the Roman emperor. It was the headquarters for many ancient guilds: the potters', tanners', weavers', robe makers', and dyers' guilds. It was the center of the dyeing industry. This is where the labor unions must have originated! Lydia, the seller of purple, who in Philippi became Paul's first convert in Europe, came from here (see Acts 16:14). That purple color spoken of is what we know today as "Turkey red"— and I mean that color is red. The dye was taken from a plant that grows in that area. Apollo, the sun god, was worshiped here as Tyrimnos.

> **And unto the angel of the church in Thyatira write; These things saith the Son of God, who hath his eyes like unto a flame of fire, and his feet are like fine brass [Rev. 2:18].**

This pictures the Son of God in judgment. His eyes are like a flame of fire, searching them out, and His feet are like burnished brass, which represents judgment. Christ is judging this church.

However, He has words of commendation for this church. If you think that the Roman church during the Dark Ages is to be condemned wholeheartedly, you need to check up on the history of it. The Lord Jesus says,

> **I know thy works, and charity, and service, and faith, and thy patience, and thy works; and the last to be more than the first [Rev. 2:19].**

Christ has six words of commendation for the church of the Dark Ages in which were many true believers who had a personal love of Christ which was manifested in works. Works are actually credentials of true believers. James says, "Yea, a man may say, Thou hast faith, and I have works: shew me thy faith without thy works, and I will shew thee my faith by my works" (James 2:18).

The six words of commendation are:

1. "Works" were the credentials of real believers. There were many who lived spotless lives and by their good works "adorned the doctrine."

2. "Love." It was a church in which there was love, in spite of the fact that it had gone in for ritualism. There were some wonderful saints of God during that period: Bernard of Clairvaux, Peter Waldo, John Wycliffe, John Huss, Savonarola, and Anselm were all men in the Roman church.

3. "Faith." Though it is placed after works and love in this instance, it is the mainspring that turns the hands of works and love.

4. "Ministry" is service.

5. "Patience" is endurance in those days of darkness.

6. "Thy last works are more than the first." In this church, works increased rather than diminished.

All six virtues are produced within the believer by the Holy Spirit. There is one frightful charge of condemnation:

Notwithstanding I have a few things against thee, because thou sufferest that woman Jezebel, which calleth herself a prophetess, to teach and to seduce my servants to commit fornication, and to eat things sacrificed unto idols [Rev. 2:20].

But I have against you that you tolerate the woman (wife) Jezebel, who calls herself the prophetess, and she teaches and seduces my servants to commit fornication and to eat things sacrificed to idols.

Jezebel had brought paganism into the northern kingdom of Israel. And evidently there was in the local church at Thyatira a woman who had a reputation as a teacher and prophetess who was the counterpart of Jezebel, the consort of Ahab.

And concerning the historical period of the Dark Ages which the church at Thyatira represents, pagan practices and idolatry were mingled with Christian works and worship. The papacy was elevated to a place of secular power under Gregory I (A.D. 590), and later by Gregory VII, better known as Hildebrand (A.D. 1073–1085). The introduction of rituals and church doctrine supplanted personal faith in Jesus Christ. Worship of the Virgin and Child and the Mass were made a definite part of the church service. Purgatory became a positive doctrine, and Mass was said for the dead. The spurious documents labeled Donation of Constantine and Decretals of Isidore were circulated to give power and rulership to the pope.

As Jezebel killed Naboth and persecuted God's prophets, so the Roman church instituted the Inquisition during this period.

"Seduce" means a fundamental departure from the truth, according to Vincent. Jezebel stands in sharp contrast to Lydia, who came from Thyatira. Jezebel is merely a forerunner of the apostate church, as we shall see in chapter 17.

And I gave her space to repent of her fornication; and she repented not [Rev. 2:21].

"Space" is time. The Lord Jesus Christ has patiently dealt with this false system for over a thousand years, and there has been no real change down through the centuries in this system. In fact, Rome boasts that she never changes—semper idem, always the same.

Behold, I will cast her into a bed, and them that commit adultery with her into great tribulation, except they repent of their deeds [Rev. 2:22].

"Great tribulation" could refer to the persecution which Rome is enduring under communism. Or it may mean the Great Tribulation into which the apostate church will go.

"Their deeds" should be translated her deeds.

And I will kill her children with death; and all the churches shall know that I am he which searcheth the reins and hearts: and I will give unto every one of you according to your works [Rev. 2:23].

"Children" are those who were brought up under this system.

"And I will kill her children with death" is translated by Vincent: "Let them be put to death with death," referring to the second death.

"All the churches" refers to the church of all the ages.

"The reins" means literally the kidneys and refers to the total psychological makeup—the thoughts, the feelings, the purposes. When He searches the reins and the hearts, it means that He searches our entire beings.

> **But unto you I say, and unto the rest in Thyatira, as many as have not this doctrine, and which have not known the depths of Satan, as they speak; I will put upon you none other burden [Rev. 2:24].**

> *But I say to you, to the rest in Thyatira, who do not hold this doctrine, which are of those who have not known the depths of Satan, as they say, I will put upon you none other burden (weight).*

The church in Thyatira, we know from history, had a very brief existence because it went down with the city when it was captured by the enemy.

"The depths of Satan" perhaps refers to a gnostic sect known as the Ophites who worshiped the serpent. They made a parody of Paul's words. All heresy boasts of superior spiritual perception, and that is what this group did.

> **But that which ye have already hold fast till I come [Rev. 2:25].**

Obviously, Christ is beginning to say to His church, "I am coming to take you out, and because of this, you should stand fast for Me."

> **And he that overcometh, and keepeth my works unto the end, to him will I give power over the nations [Rev. 2:26].**

The works of Christ are in contrast to the works of Jezebel. The works of Christ are wrought by the Holy Spirit. We overcome by faith and not by effort.

"I give power over the nations" was explained by Paul when he wrote to the Corinthian believers: "Do ye not know that the saints shall judge the world? . . . (1 Cor. 6:2).

> And he shall rule them with a rod of iron; as the vessels of a potter shall they be broken to shivers: even as I received of my Father [Rev. 2:27].

This is a reference to the millennial reign of Christ in which believers are to share.

> And I will give him the morning star [Rev. 2:28].

Christ is the Bright and Morning Star (see Rev. 22:16). Christ's coming for His own at the Rapture is the hope of the church. "Looking for that blessed hope, and the glorious appearing of the great God and our Saviour Jesus Christ" (Titus 2:13).

> He that hath an ear, let him hear what the Spirit saith unto the churches [Rev. 2:29].

The children of Jezebel will not hear, but the true children of the Lord Jesus will hear, for the Holy Spirit opens the "blood-tipped ear."

CHAPTER 3

THEME: The church in the world—continued

CHRIST'S LETTER TO THE CHURCH IN SARDIS

In the panorama of church history, Sardis represents the Protestant church during the period between A.D. 1517 and approximately A.D. 1800. It began, I believe, when Martin Luther nailed his *Ninety-Five Theses* onto the chapel door of the church at Wittenburg, Germany. It is an era which started with the Reformation and takes us into the beginning of the great missionary movement in the history of the church.

Sardis was the capital of the great kingdom of Lydia and one of the oldest and most important cities of Asia Minor. It was located inland and built on a small, elevated plateau which rises sharply above the Hermus Valley. On all sides but one the rock walls are smooth, nearly perpendicular and absolutely unscalable. The only access is on the southern side by a very steep and difficult path. One time when I was there, another preacher and I tried to make the climb. He went farther than I did, but we both gave up long before we reached the top.

As the civilization and the commerce grew more complex, the high plateau became too small, and a lower city was built chiefly on the west side of the original city. The old city was used as an acropolis. Actually this made it a double city, and it was called by the plural noun *Sardeis* or *Sardis*. The plain was well watered by the Pactolus River. It became the center of the carpet industry and was noted for its wealth. Coins were first minted there. Its last prince was the wealthy Croesus who was captured by Cyrus. He was considered the wealthiest man in the world, and everything he touched seemed to turn to gold. Sardis was ruled by the Persians, by Alexander, by Antiochus the Great, and finally by the Romans. It was destroyed by an earthquake during the reign of Tiberius.

In our day the ruins of the temple of Cybele and also of the temple of Apollo can still be seen. It is one of the few double temples that you will find in the world. Cybele was known as Diana in Ephesus, but when you get inland, she becomes a nature goddess. She was the goddess of the moon, and Apollo was the god of the sun—they were brother and sister. This was a very corrupt worship, much like the worship of Diana at Ephesus.

Extensive excavations have taken place at Sardis. They are rebuilding the gymnasium and also the synagogue. And they have dug up the Roman road that is there. The thing that thrilled me when I looked at that road was that I knew the apostle Paul had walked up and down it.

> **And unto the angel of the church in Sardis write; These things saith he that hath the seven Spirits of God, and the seven stars; I know thy works, that thou hast a name that thou livest, and art dead [Rev. 3:1].**

"These things saith he that hath the seven Spirits of God, and the seven stars." He presents Himself to the church at Sardis as the One having the seven Spirits of God; that is, He is the One who sent the Holy Spirit into the world.

As we have seen, Sardis represents the Protestant church. My friend, the church today needs the Spirit of God working in it. We think we need methods, and we have all kinds of Band-Aid courses for believers in which you put on a little Band-Aid, and it will solve all your problems. What we really need to do is to get to the person of Christ whom only the Holy Spirit can make real and living to us. This is the thing Protestantism needs today.

Following the dark night of the Dark Ages, the Holy Spirit was still in the world doing His work. He moved in the hearts of men like Martin Luther, John Calvin, John Knox, and many, many others.

"I know thy works." This is the word of commendation. Remember that the Reformation recovered the doctrine of justification by faith, and this faith produced works.

"That thou hast a name that thou livest, and art dead." Protestantism today, as a whole, has a name that it lives, but it is dead. Many Protestant churches today are just going through the form. They are building all the time, and people are coming, especially on Sunday mornings. But there are not many at the midweek service, when they really ought to come to hear the Word of God. "Thou hast a name that thou livest, and art dead." This is a frightful condemnation and is a picture of Protestantism today.

We need to recognize that all of the truth was not recovered by the Reformation. For example, I believe that the doctrine of eschatology, prophecy, is just now being developed in our own day.

> **Be watchful, and strengthen the things which remain, that are ready to die: for I have not found thy works perfect before God [Rev. 3:2].**

Let me give you my translation of this verse:

> *Wake up and watch out and establish the things that remain which were about to die, for I have found no works of thine fulfilled (perfected) before my God.*

This is the second word of condemnation, and it is a word of warning which had particular meaning in Sardis. As I have said, Sardis was located on the top of a mountain. It had one entrance on the southern side which was the only way you could get into the city in the old days. Therefore, all that Sardis had to do was to put a detail at that one place to watch the city. But on two occasions in their history they had been invaded by their enemies because they had felt secure, believing that the hill was impregnable, and the guard went to sleep on the job. In 549 B.C. the Median soldiers of Cyrus scaled the parapet, and then again in 218 B.C. Antiochus the Great captured Sardis because a Cretan slipped over the walls while the sentries were careless. What the Lord says to this church at Sardis is this: "You wake up and watch out!" This was embarrassing because of the two occasions in their history when they had been caught napping. He says to the church, "Don't you go to sleep!"

Protestantism, as a whole, has turned away from looking for the coming of Jesus Christ, and they have built up these systems that certain things must be fulfilled before He can come. My friend, it is *tissue-thin* from where we are right now to the coming of Christ for His church. He could come the next moment or tomorrow. Don't say that I said He is coming tomorrow because I don't know. It may be a hundred years, but, my friend, His imminent return is what we are to look for. Sardis didn't know when the enemy was coming, and we don't know when Christ is coming—we have no way of knowing at all.

In view of the fact that the Rapture could take place at any moment, the church is to be alert. The date is not set, nor even the period in which He will come, and the reason for that is that the church is to be constantly on the alert for His coming—"Looking for that blessed hope . . ." (Titus 2:13). You see, anyone can make ready for a fixed hour, but you must *always* be ready for an unexpected hour. The Lord Jesus is saying to Protestantism that they are constantly to be on the alert.

"For I have not found thy works perfect before God." Protestantism did recover the authority of the Word of God, the total depravity of man, and justification by faith, but there are many other things that they did not recover. The Reformation was not a return to the apostolic church.

Remember therefore how thou hast received and heard, and hold fast, and repent. If therefore thou shalt not watch, I will come on thee as a thief, and thou shalt not know what hour I will come upon thee [Rev. 3:3].

"Remember therefore how thou hast received and heard, and hold fast, and repent." The idea is that they were to hold fast to these things because they were about to die. The great truths which were recovered in the Reformation are being lost. For instance, the Protestant church, by and large, has lost the authority of the Word of God. Rather than holding to the doctrine of the total depravity of man, many of our conservative churches are improving and using cosmetics on the carnal nature, thinking that somehow or another you can get up a few little rules and regulations which are going to enable you to live the

Christian life. Also, the great doctrine of justification by faith has been pretty much abandoned, and a legalistic message is given that you have to do something in order to be saved. These are the things which characterize Protestantism today; it is very far from its original position.

"If therefore thou shalt not watch, I will come on thee as a thief, and thou shalt not know what hour I will come upon thee." As we have seen, Sardis was built high upon a mountaintop which was impossible to scale except at one point. There is so much erosion of the soil in Turkey that two thousand years ago—in the days of Paul and John—the mountain was much higher and even more inaccessible than it is today. In spite of that, there were these two occasions when enemy soldiers gained entrance to the city. This was very embarrassing to this city—two times it was captured because the guard went to sleep. The Lord says to the church at Sardis, "Don't you go to sleep. Wake up and watch out." He could come at any moment. The people of Sardis did not know when the enemy was coming, and we do not know when the Lord Jesus is coming.

Thou hast a few names even in Sardis which have not defiled their garments; and they shall walk with me in white: for they are worthy [Rev. 3:4].

But thou hast a few names (persons) in Sardis that did not besmirch (defile) their Christian life (garments); and they shall walk with me in white (garments); for they are worthy.

In Israel it was never the corporate body of the total national life but always a remnant that was true to God. Here the church is told, "You have a few." In Luke 12:32 the Lord called His church "little flock." Protestantism today has its saints who love the Word, who are faithful to Him even in these days, and who stand by the Word of God. They do not engage in sin-defiling activities, nor are they engaged in fleshly activity.

Protestantism has produced some great men, and I will mention some, although I am going to leave out a great many. I think of the Reformation leaders: Martin Luther and John Calvin stand out, head and shoulders, above all others. Of course, there was John Knox, a great man of God who did so much for Scotland. Later on, there was John Bunyan, the great Baptist who wrote *Pilgrim's Progress*, which tells of his own life and how God marvelously saved him. John Wesley was the founder of the Methodist church. God marvelously saved that man and used him in such a way that he is given credit by historians for saving England from the revolution which destroyed France and prevented it from ever becoming a first-rate nation again. Wesley has been called the greatest Englishman of all. He certainly did more for that country than any other Englishman who has ever lived. Then there was a man like John Moffatt, the Scotchman who went to Africa, and David Livingstone who first opened up that continent. William Carey went to India and later was followed by a sickly young man by the name of Henry Martyn. Finally, I always like to include Titus Coan, who led the greatest revival since Pentecost out in the Hawaiian Islands.

Protestantism has had some names who didn't defile themselves and were true to the Word of God. There are quite a few such men living today, but I wouldn't dare to begin to name them because of the fact that I would be apt to leave some out who ought to be included.

Protestantism has certainly produced some great men of God. Romanism did the same thing, even during the Dark Ages, but that does not mean to commend the system. The system of Romanism and the system of Protestantism, as they are revealed in the great denominations which have departed from the faith, to me are the organizations which will eventually bring in the apostate church because they have departed from the great tenets and doctrines of the Christian faith.

Verse 5 is a difficult passage of Scripture—

He that overcometh, the same shall be clothed in white raiment; and I will not blot out his name out of the book

of life, but I will confess his name before my Father, and before his angels [Rev. 3:5].

"He that overcometh." The one who overcomes by the blood of Christ, of course, never does it because of his own strength, cleverness, or ability.

Now He makes this statement which has caused the difficulty in understanding: "I will not blot out his name out of the book of life, but I will confess his name before my Father, and before his angels." It is interesting to note that in the genealogies there are only two books which are identified: (1) "the book of the generations of Adam" (see Gen. 5:1)—we are all in that book, but it is a book of death—and (2) "the book of the generation of Jesus Christ" (see Matt. 1:1). The phrase, "the book of the generation," is an unusual expression. It occurs only in connection with Adam and then in connection with Christ.

The book of the generation of Jesus Christ is the Book of Life. I believe that you get into that book by faith in Christ. This, then, raises the question here: Is it possible for you to be in the Book of Life and then have your name blotted out? Can you lose your salvation? If that is true, then the Lord Jesus should not have said, "And I give unto them eternal life; and they shall never perish, neither shall any man pluck them out of my hand" (John 10:28). Again and again throughout Scripture we have the assurance given to us of our salvation.

I would like to give you now an excerpt from Dr. John Walvoord's book *The Revelation of Jesus Christ,* which is a very good explanation of what is meant in this verse:

Some have indicated that there is no explicit statement here that anybody will have his name blotted out, but rather the promise that his name will not be blotted out because of his faith in Christ. The implication, however, is that such is a possibility. On the basis of this some have considered the book of life not as the roll of those who are saved but rather a list of those for whom Christ died, that is, all humanity who have possessed physical life. As they come to maturity and are faced

with the responsibility of accepting or rejecting Christ, their
names are blotted out if they fail to receive Jesus Christ as Saviour; whereas those who do accept Christ as Saviour are con-
firmed in their position in the book of life, and their names are
confessed before the Father and the heavenly angels.

I think that that is a good, sound interpretation.

In Revelation there is a great importance placed on this book (see
Rev. 13:8; 17:8; 20:12, 15; 21:27; 22:19). In these references the
thought is that there are those whose names are recorded and those
whose names are not recorded in the Book of Life. We will talk about it
again, especially when we get to the last reference in the twenty-
second chapter.

Some have identified the two books in chapter 20, verse 12, as the
book of profession and the book of reality. They hold that names are
erased from the book of profession but not from the book of reality.
Others have suggested that all names are placed in the Book of Life at
the beginning, but some are removed. A person's lack of decision for
or rejection of Christ causes his name to be removed at the time of
death. Both of these views propose serious objections as well as having good points to commend them.

I am confident that the whole thought is simply that it was amazing that anyone in Sardis would be saved but that there were some
whose names He said would not be blotted out of the Book of Life. He
didn't say that anybody had been blotted out; He just said that even in
Sardis there would be some saved. May I say to you, the important
thing is whether or not your name is written in the Lamb's Book of
Life. I do not believe that after you are saved you would ever be able to
lose that salvation.

**He that hath an ear, let him hear what the Spirit saith
unto the churches [Rev. 3:6].**

This, again, is the blood-tipped ear that needs to hear the voice of the
Spirit speaking through the Word of God the message of Christ to His
church today.

CHRIST'S LETTER TO THE CHURCH
IN PHILADELPHIA

The church in Philadelphia represents what I call the revived church, dating from approximately the beginning of the nineteenth century to the Rapture. This is the church that has turned back to the Word of God. Today in Protestantism and also in the Roman Catholic Church, there are multitudes of people who are turning to the Word of God. Mail which I receive from all over the world indicates that there are people wanting to hear the Word of God and who are hungry for it. This period is pictured in the church of Philadelphia.

I have visited the city of Philadelphia, and it is today a rather prosperous little Turkish town. It is located in a very beautiful valley that is inland a great distance, about 125–150 miles from the coast. The valley is a very wide one which runs north and south, and the Cogamis River of that valley is a tributary of the Hermus River. The city was built on four or five hills in a picturesque setting. Today it is spread out a great deal, and it is a typical Turkish town.

Philadelphia is in an area that is subject to earthquakes. The great population that was in that area left primarily because of earthquakes and, of course, because of warfare. When Tamerlane and the other great pagan leaders came out of the East, it was a time when all those who were left were slaughtered. Therefore, today no descendants of the original population are there. However, this city has had continuous habitation from its very beginning.

This city was like a Greek island out in Lydia, out in the Anatolian country, an area which the Greeks considered to be heathen and pagan—the Greek word for it was *barbarian*. In fact, anyone who was not a Greek was considered a barbarian in those days. The Lydian language was spoken there at first, but by the time of the apostles, the Greek language had taken over, and it was a typical Greek colony. This was the outpost of Greek culture in a truly Asiatic and Anatolian atmosphere. It was called a "little Athens" because of the fact that it was in this area and yet was truly Greek.

It was a fortress city used to waylay the enemy who would come in to destroy the greater cities like Ephesus and Smyrna and Pergamum—

those were the three great cities. These other cities were largely fortress cities where garrisons were stationed either to stop the enemy or delay him as he marched toward the western coast.

Philadelphia is in a country where erosion is at work; the soil is quite alluvial, but it is very fertile soil. Beautiful laurel trees, many flowers—I noticed that they are growing just about everything that is imaginable. It was particularly celebrated for its excellent wine. Great vineyards covered the surrounding hills, and the head of Bacchus was imprinted on their coins.

The city did not get its name, as so many seem to think, from the Bible. Actually, the city got its name because of the love that Attalus II had for his brother Eumenes who was king of Pergamum. Attalus had a great love and loyalty for his brother, and because of that it is called "the city of brotherly love."

In A.D. 17 a great earthquake struck this city and totally destroyed it. The same earthquake totally destroyed Sardis and many other Lydian cities throughout that area. Tiberius, the emperor at that time, allocated a vast sum of money for the rebuilding of these cities, and they were then restored.

This is the one church besides Smyrna for which our Lord had no word of condemnation. Why? Because it had turned to the Word of God. It is interesting concerning the two churches which He did not condemn that the places are still in existence, although the churches have disappeared. However, in Philadelphia there is something quite interesting about which I would like to tell you. First of all, there are the remains of a Byzantine church, which reveals that Christianity was active there up until the twelfth or thirteenth century. The people who are caretakers of that area today must be Christians. Although I could not converse with them, they very graciously brought me a pitcher of water and a dipper on the very warm day I was there. The man and his wife who brought it were all smiles. I couldn't talk to them, and they couldn't talk to me, but I felt that we did communicate something of Christian love.

The remains of that Byzantine church are still there, but that is not the pillar that is mentioned in verse 12, although many believe that it is, and that is where the guides take the tours. However, before my first trip there, I had seen a picture of a big amphitheater in Adam's *Biblical Backgrounds;* so I told my guide that I wanted to go up there on the side of the hill. The amphitheater was no longer there, but there was a Turkish coffee shop where my guide talked to a man. He said that there had been an amphitheater but it was totally destroyed except for one pillar. I have a picture of that pillar which is hidden away under the trees. Why did the Turkish government get rid of that amphitheater? I'll tell you why: The Seljuk Turks brutally killed the Christians in Philadelphia, and they wanted to get rid of every vestige of that old civilization. Today they would rather that you and I forget about it.

Philadelphia is the place where Christian and Saracen fought during the Crusades, and in 1922 Turkey and Greece fought in Philadelphia. There are apparently a few Christians there today, as I have suggested, but they are under cover because they would be severely persecuted.

The church of Philadelphia continued into the thirteenth century. This church was in a very strategic area to be a missionary church, and that is actually what it was. I have labeled it the revived church because it returned to the Word of God and began to teach the Word of God.

This represents something that I think we see in Protestantism today. It began back in the last century and has gained since then, so that Bible teaching is not something that is new, by any means, but it has certainly become rather popular today. We feel very definitely that our Bible-teaching radio program has come in on the crest of a wave of interest in the Word of God.

> **And to the angel of the church in Philadelphia write; These things saith he that is holy, he that is true, he that hath the key of David, he that openeth, and no man shutteth; and shutteth, and no man openeth [Rev. 3:7].**

"And to the angel of the church in Philadelphia write." The angel is the human messenger, the pastor, of the church. This is the Lord's method in all of these churches.

"These things saith he that is holy, he that is true, he that hath the key of David, he that openeth, and no man shutteth; and shutteth, and no man openeth." In each of these messages, the Lord always draws something from that vision of Himself as the glorified Christ, our Great High Priest, in chapter 1. Here He reminds them that He is holy. He was holy at His birth, He was holy at His death, and He is holy today in His present priestly office. He was so called at His birth when the angel said to Mary, ". . . therefore also that *holy* thing which shall be born of thee shall be called the Son of God" (Luke 1:35, italics mine). And in His death He was holy. We are told in Acts 2:27: "Because thou wilt not leave my soul in hell, neither wilt thou suffer thine *Holy One* to see corruption" (italics mine). He was holy in His death and in His resurrection. What a marvelous thing this is! He is also holy today in His high priestly office. "For such an high priest became us, who is *holy*, harmless, undefiled, separate from sinners, and made higher than the heavens" (Heb. 7:26, italics mine).

"He that is true." John 14:6 tells us, ". . . I am the way, the truth, and the life. . . ." True means "genuine" with an added note of perfection and completeness. Moses did not give the true bread; Christ is the true Bread (see John 6:32–35).

"He that hath the key of David." This is different from the keys of hades and death which we saw in chapter 1, verse 18. This speaks of His regal claims as the Ruler of this universe. "He shall be great, and shall be called the Son of the Highest: and the Lord God shall give unto him the throne of his father David: and he shall reign over the house of Jacob for ever; and of his kingdom there shall be no end" (Luke 1:32–33). He will sit on the throne of David in the Millennium, but today He is sovereign, sitting at His Father's right hand, waiting for His enemies to be made His footstool.

"He that openeth, and no man shutteth; and shutteth, and no man openeth." He is the One today who is able to open and to close, and because of that He is a comfort to us (see Matt. 28:18–20).

I know thy works: behold, I have set before thee an open door, and no man can shut it: for thou hast a little

strength, and hast kept my word, and hast not denied my name [Rev. 3:8].

I know thy works: behold, I have given thee a door opened, which none can shut, for thou hast a little strength [Gr.: dunamin], and didst keep my word, and didst not deny my name.

This is the verse that we have taken as the maxim for our "Thru the Bible" radio program. We began with it at the first, and it means a great deal to us.

The church at Philadelphia was the one which was true to the Word of God. In our day the church which it represents could not be called the Protestant church or the Roman Catholic church or any other church. Actually, it represents all churches the world over— regardless of their labels—which still remain true to the Word of God.

The Lord commends the Philadelphian church on seven counts:

1. "I know thy works." The Lord Jesus is looking for fruit; He is looking for works in the lives of believers. "For by grace are ye saved through faith; and that not of yourselves: it is the gift of God: not of works, lest any man should boast. For we are his workmanship, created in Christ Jesus unto good works, which God hath before ordained that we should walk in them" (Eph. 2:8–10).

My friend, there is something wrong with your faith if it doesn't produce works. Good, old, practical, camel-kneed James was a great man of prayer who said, ". . . shew me thy faith without thy works, and I will shew thee my faith by my works" (James 2:18). "Works" are not works of law but works of faith. Calvin said, "Faith alone saves, but faith that saves is not alone." Saving faith produces works.

2. "Behold, I have set before thee an open door, and no man can shut it." This could be a door to the joy of the Lord or to a knowledge of the Scriptures. I personally believe that it is a door to the knowledge of the Scriptures, which means that if He opens the door, He intends for you to move in because He will open a door of opportunity for witnessing and for proclaiming the Word of God. I believe that both go together.

3. "For thou hast a little strength [dunamin]." *Dunamin* is the Greek word from which we get our English word *dynamite*. He says, "You have a *little* power." This was a humble group of believers which did not have impressive numbers, buildings, or programs. I get a little weary today hearing every Christian group making reports. Even here at "Thru the Bible" we like to tell you how many radio stations our broadcast is heard on. My, how we like to talk about those things! My friend, that type of thing is not worth anything. We like to talk about the hundreds of letters we receive from those who have accepted Christ—that's nothing. The important thing is whether or not we are getting out the Word of God. He will do the counting. God has His own computer which is registering all this, and He tells us that we had better not. The apostle Paul said, "I don't even judge myself" (see 1 Cor. 4:3). Why not? In effect he is saying, "I may report too many converts. I may speak 'evangelistically' and give you a wrong figure. I may look at this a little differently than God does. I need to wait until I get into His presence for the accurate rendering of it."

4. "And hast kept my word." In a day when there was a denial of the inspiration of the Scriptures, this church believed the Bible to be the authoritative, inspired Word of God. A twentieth-century theologian, of course of the liberal ranks, stated that no intelligent person could believe in the verbal inspiration of the Bible. Well, that sure puts me in a bad light! I am, therefore, not an intelligent person because I do believe in the inspiration of the Bible—that is, *if* his definition is right, but I do not think he is right even about that.

5. "And hast not denied my name." In a day when the deity of Christ is blatantly denied by seminary and pulpit, here is a group of believers who have remained true to Him by proclaiming the God-man and His substitutionary death for sinners.

This church in Philadelphia has been labeled many things. Some have called it the missionary church; some have called it the serving church; some have called it a live church—all of these are accurate. I personally like to call it the revived church or the Bible-believing church; it is the Bible church. The thing that the Lord Jesus emphasizes is this: "Thou . . . hast kept my word, and hast not denied my name." In that day of unbelief and skepticism, the Lord Jesus is commending this church because it has kept His Word. This is the church that got out the Word of God and, as far as we know, this church lasted longer than any other of the seven churches mentioned here Until the thirteenth century, it had a continuous existence. It was destroyed by the Seljuk Turks when they came in and brutally murdered all the believers who were left in this church. It was also a missionary church. It is the belief now that the fact that Christianity penetrated into India as early as it did was because this church had sent out missionaries.

> **Behold, I will make them of the synagogue of Satan, which say they are Jews, and are not, but do lie; behold, I will make them to come and worship before thy feet, and to know that I have loved thee [Rev. 3:9].**

Let me give you my translation:

> *Behold I give of the synagogue of Satan, of them that say they are Jews, and are not, but lie. Behold, I will make them that they shall come and worship before your feet, and to know that I have loved you.*

The remnant of Israel which was being saved had left the synagogue by this time. They had given up the Law as a means of salvation and sanctification. Those who continued in the synagogue were now in a false religion. As Paul makes it clear, ". . . For they are not all Israel, which are of Israel" (Rom. 9:6)—they were no longer true Jews. He considered the true Israelite to be the one who had turned to Christ.

Ignatius, according to Trench and reported by Vincent, refers to a logical situation where converts from Judaism preached the faith they once despised. By the way, the Roman Empire used Jews for the purpose of colonizing. They would send a regular colony of them into a foreign area, as they did into this section, and this is the reason there were so many Jews there.

6. "Behold, I will make them to come and worship before thy feet, and to know that I have loved thee." The Lord Jesus says here that He

will make the enemies of the Philadelphian church to know that He loves this church. This is His sixth point of commendation.

> **Because thou hast kept the word of my patience, I also will keep thee from the hour of temptation, which shall come upon all the world, to try them that dwell upon the earth [Rev. 3:10].**
>
> *Because thou didst keep the word of my patience, I, also, will keep you out of (from) the hour of the trial, which is (about) to come upon the whole inhabited world to test (try) them that dwell upon the earth.*

7. This last commendation is that this church kept the Word of Christ in patience. This is evidently the patient waiting for the coming of Christ for His own (see 2 Thess. 3:5). It has been in the present century that the doctrines of eschatology have been developed more than in all previous centuries combined. During the past forty years, there has been a revival of interest, both in Europe and in America, in fact, all over the world, relative to the second coming of Christ. Even the liberals talk about it now and then.

"Because thou hast kept the word of my patience." I believe that God today is still patient with a world that has rejected His Word. It is not like it was back in the days of Noah. They didn't have the written Word of God, yet God judged them; they did have a man bringing the message to them. But today we *do* have the Word of God. There is a Gideon Bible in practically every hotel and motel room throughout the world. In the different countries of Europe, Asia, and Africa, I find that the Word of God has penetrated all of these areas. The Philadelphian church is the church that believed in the Word of God.

"I also will keep thee from the hour of temptation, which shall come upon all the world, to try them that dwell upon the earth." Christ's final word of encouragement to His church is that it will not pass through the Great Tribulation. The church is to be removed from the world (see 1 Thess. 4:13–18), which is its comfort and hope (see Titus 2:13). Such is the patient waiting of the church ". . . who through faith and patience inherit the promises" (Heb. 6:12). The church is not anticipating the Great Tribulation with all of its judgment (see John 5:24; Rev. 13:1–8, 11–17), but rather it is looking for Him to come.

"The hour of temptation" is definitely a reference to the Great Tribulation—it's worldwide. After the preliminaries are put down in chapters 4—5, in chapters 6—19 you have presented the Great Tribulation Period. This is the period that He says is coming upon all the world to test those that are upon the earth.

"I also will keep thee from the hour of temptation." He says that He will keep them not only from that awful holocaust that is coming on this earth, that period of judgment, but also from the hour of temptation. Therefore, this is to my judgment a complete deliverance. When he says, "keep thee from the hour," I have translated it, "keep thee out of the hour of trial." By any stretch of the imagination, you could not say that this church is going through the Great Tribulation Period. I believe that the period of the Philadelphian church continues right on through to the rapture of the church. This is the church which will go out at the time of the Rapture.

The church of Laodicea, as we shall see, is an organization which will continue on in the world, although the Lord gives a marvelous invitation to it, and many even in that Laodicean church will turn to Christ and be taken out at the time of the Rapture. But there is a church that goes through the Great Tribulation Period, and that is the apostate church, the church of Laodicea.

What we have here, therefore, is the coming of Christ to take His own out of the world and His promise to the church of Philadelphia that it will not go through that particular period that is coming on the earth.

I would like to give here another quotation from Dr. John Walvoord's book, *The Revelation of Jesus Christ:*

If the rapture had occurred in the first century preceding the tribulation which the book of Revelation describes, they were assured of deliverance. By contrast, those sealed out of the twelve tribes of Israel in 7:4 clearly go through the time of trouble. This implies the rapture of the church before the time of trouble referred to as the great tribulation. Such a promise of deliverance to them would seemingly have been impossible if the rapture of the church were delayed until the end of the trib- ulation prior to the second coming of Christ and the establish- ment of the kingdom.

Christ says to the church—

> Behold, I come quickly: hold that fast which thou hast, that no man take thy crown [Rev. 3:11].

"Behold, I come quickly." "Quickly" does not mean soon. Rather, it has the idea of suddenness and an air of expectation; that is, He will come at a time they know not. It does not mean He is coming immedi- ately, but His coming will be sudden. This is the promise that is the hope of the church. Actually, the church is not looking for the Great Tribulation Period. Nowhere are you told that you are to gird up your loins, grit your teeth, and clench your fists because the Great Tribula- tion is coming and you are certainly going through it! He never said that, but "Looking for that blessed hope, and the glorious appearing of the great God and our Saviour Jesus Christ" (Titus 2:13).

Let me say again that the Philadelphian church represents the re- vived church, the church that has returned to the Word of God. It is this church that is to be raptured, His true church, and I do not think you can put them in any denomination or any local church. They are scattered throughout the world today, and you will find some of them belonging to some very funny organizations. I don't understand that, but that is apparently none of my business; that is something they will have to straighten out with the Lord.

> Him that overcometh will I make a pillar in the temple of my God, and he shall go no more out: and I will write upon him the name of my God, and the name of the city of my God, which is new Jerusalem, which cometh down out of heaven from my God: and I will write upon him my new name [Rev. 3:12].

There are two pillars in Philadelphia today. One is that of the Byzantine church, which I do not think is the reference here. But there is also a pillar on the side of the hill, hidden among those cedar and laurel trees. That pillar is all that remains of the city of John's day. "Him that overcometh will I make a pillar in the temple of my God." The church down here was destroyed, but the permanent pillar is up yonder.

"And I will write upon him the name of my God, and the name of the city of my God, which is new Jerusalem, which cometh down out of heaven from my God: and I will write upon him my new name." This is the passport and visa of the believer which will enable him, as a citizen of heaven, to pass freely upon this earth or anywhere in God's universe. He is a pillar to "go no more out," but with God's passport he is to go everywhere. Although this is paradoxical, it is all wonderfully and blessedly true.

"I will write upon him my new name." This is *His* name. We do not have a new name; rather, He is saying that He has a new name for Himself that He will give to us. This new name is a personal relationship we will have with Him.

He that hath an ear, let him hear what the Spirit saith unto the churches [Rev. 3:13].

The Lord has a message that He gives to each one of these churches. It applied to that local church, but it also applies to us today.

CHRIST'S LETTER TO THE CHURCH IN LAODICEA

The letter of Christ to the church in Laodicea is the last of these seven letters. Sir William Ramsay calls Laodicea "the city of compromise." This city was founded by Antiochus II (261–246 B.C.). It had a Seleucid foundation. Seleucus was one of the generals of Alexander who took Syria. Lysimachus took Asia Minor, but apparently Seleucus moved over into his territory and took some of his ground, including this city.

Laodicea was about forty miles east and inland from Ephesus on the Lycus River, which flows into the Maeander River. It is located at what is known as the "Gate of Phrygia." Out of the Oriental East, the great camel caravans came down through the Gate of Phrygia and through Laodicea. This road came out of the East and went to Ephesus, to Miletus, and also up to what is called Izmir today but was Smyrna in that day. Laodicea was in a spectacular place, a great valley. Today its ruins are largely covered up with the growth of what looks like wild oats. Its name means "justice of the people." It was named for Laodice, the wife of Antiochus. Although there were several cities which bore this name, this was the most famous one of all.

Between Laodicea and going on up to the Phrygian mountains, there was in this valley a great Anatolian temple of the Phrygian god, Men Karou. This was the primitive god of that area. The temple was the very center of all society, administration, trade, and religion. There was a great market there, and strangers came from everywhere to trade. I suppose that the large market in Istanbul today is very similar to it.

Laodicea was a place of great wealth, of commerce, and of Greek culture. It was a place of science and of literature. It boasted an excellent medical school which, again, was very primitive and actually very heathen. Here is where they developed what was known in the Roman world as Phrygian powder, a salve for the ears and the eyes. Laodicea was also a center of industry with extensive banking operations. Cicero held court here. It is said that he brought notes here to be cashed in this city. Jupiter, or Zeus, was the object of worship in Laodicea.

The city was finally abandoned because of earthquakes. The very impressive ruins of two Roman theaters, a large stadium, and three early Christian churches are still there. The city itself has not been excavated. In other words, these ruins which I have mentioned protrude through all the debris and wild growth that is there. I have heard that there is an American foundation which has set aside two to three million dollars to excavate Laodicea. I would love to join that excavation for it would be very worthwhile.

Laodicea was a place of great commerce where they made clothing. As you stand on the ruins of Laodicea, you can look around at the nearby hills and see where Colosse is located and also Hierapolis, where there are springs. The greatest ruins are not in Colosse or Laodicea but in Hierapolis. The hills have a very funny color. The people took the clay from those hills, put it with a spikenard, and made it into a salve for the eyes and ears. This salve was shipped all over the Roman Empire. Today the chemical analysis reveals that there is nothing healing in that clay at all, but somebody made good money at it in that day. We like to think we are civilized today, but there is a lot of medicine on the market that won't do you a bit of good; yet we are buying it just as fast as we can because of high-pressure advertising. We had better not criticize these people too much—but the Lord Jesus did. He is going to tell them that they had better get the real eye salve that will open their eyes.

And unto the angel of the church of the Laodiceans write; These things saith the Amen, the faithful and true witnes., the beginning of the creation of God [Rev. 3:14].

And to the messenger of the church in Laodicea write; These things saith the Amen, the faithful and true witness, the beginning of the creation of God.

This is the only place in Scripture where Amen is a proper name, and it is the name of Christ. In Isaiah 65:16 it should read, "the God of the amen." In Isaiah 7:9 the word *believe* is *amen*. In 2 Corinthians 1:20 we read, "For all the promises of God in him are yea, and in him Amen, unto the glory of God by us." The Lord Jesus is the Amen. He has the last word. He is the Alpha and the Omega. He is the One who is going to fulfill all the promises of God, and He lets the Laodiceans know this because this is the church that has rejected the deity of Christ. The word *Amen* is the only thing that He draws out of the vision of Himself that we had in the first chapter.

"The faithful and true witness." This reveals that the Lord Jesus Christ alone is the One who will reveal all and tell all. This is the day when it is very difficult to hear the truth. We certainly don't get it through the news media or from the government. Both our educational institutions and the military are great brain-washing institutions. Whom can you believe? Well, there is One who is the faithful and true witness even in the days of apostasy. You cannot believe the church in many instances today; the liberal church has no message for this hour.

"The beginning of the creation of God" means that He is the Creator. We live in a day when the myth of evolution, the evolutionary hypothesis, is that which is accepted. A college professor, a friend of mine, who has accepted the evolutionary hypothesis, said to me, "I want facts. I want science." I said, "Wait a minute. There are not but two explanations for the origin of this universe in which you and I live. One is *speculation*, because nobody was there to see it and nobody is able to come up with the answer. The other is *revelation*—what the Word of God has to say. Very frankly, the difference between you and me is that you accept speculation and I accept revelation. As far as I am concerned, I feel that I am on more solid ground because I have the testimony of the One who did the creating, and He ought to know something about it." The Lord Jesus is "the beginning of the creation of God."

> I know thy works, that thou art neither cold nor hot: I would thou wert cold or hot.
>
> So then because thou art lukewarm, and neither cold nor hot, I will spue thee out of my mouth [Rev. 3:15–16].

With the other churches, when the Lord Jesus said, "I know thy works," He meant good works; He was commending them for good works. But the Lord Jesus has no word of commendation for this church. All is condemnation here. Even the "works" here are not good works; they are evil works.

"That thou art neither cold nor hot: I would thou wert cold or hot." This had a background and a local meaning for the people in that day. Being down in the valley, they had difficulty getting water in Laodicea. As I stood there in the ruins, I looked south toward the Phrygian mountains, some of which are very high. I was there around the first of June, and there was still an abundance of snow on top of those mountains. The Laodiceans built an aqueduct to bring that cold water down from the mountains. When it left the mountains, it was ice cold, but by the time it made that trip all the way down the mountains to Laodicea, it was lukewarm. And lukewarm water is not very good.

Down in the valley where the Lycus River joins the Maeander River, there are hot springs. The springs are so hot that steam is produced. The Turkish government has capped it and is using it today, and I understand they intend to develop its use even more because it is there in abundance. It is the hottest water you can imagine; a lot of it is just steam. However, when they would take this hot water up to Laodicea, by the time it got there, it was no longer hot—it had become lukewarm water.

When the Lord Jesus said to the Laodicean church, "You are neither cold nor hot," they knew exactly what He was talking about. They had been drinking lukewarm water for years. Water left the mountains ice cold, and it left the springs steaming hot, but when they got it, both were lukewarm, and it was sickening. We like to put a little ice in our water, and many folk drink hot water, but lukewarm water is just not good, my friend. The Lord Jesus said that this church was neither cold nor hot and He would spew it out of His mouth.

A cold church actually means a church that has denied every cardinal doctrine of the faith. It is given over to formality and is carrying on in active opposition to the Word of God and the gospel of Christ. You find today in liberalism that they are in active opposition to the gospel of Jesus Christ. Hot speaks of those with real spiritual fervor and passion like the Christians in Ephesus, although they were even then getting away from their best love. Oh, the Spirit of God had brought them to a high pitch in their personal relationship to Christ!

But the Laodicean church was neither hot nor cold—just lukewarm. Between those positions of hot and cold, you have this lukewarm state. I would say that this is a picture of many, many churches today in the great denominations that have departed from the faith. Many churches—both in and out of these denominations—attempt to maintain a middle-of-the-road position. They do not want

to come out flatfootedly for the Word of God and for the great doctrines of the Christian faith. And at the same time, they do not want to
be known as a liberal church. So they play footsie with both groups. I
have broken fellowship with quite a few men who are extremists in
both directions, some extreme fundamentalists and some extreme liberals. And many of these men attempt to play both sides of the street.
That is a condition that is impossible. This is the thing that makes the
Lord Jesus sick. He very frankly says that He will spew them out of His
mouth.

To my judgment this middle-of-the-road position is the worst kind
of hypocrisy there is. "Thou hast a name that thou livest, and art
dead" (v. 1). "Having a form of godliness, but denying the power
thereof: from such turn away" (2 Tim. 3:5).

In its beginning Protestantism assumed the position of believing
all the great doctrines of the Christian faith. The creeds of all the great
historic denominations are wonderful creeds. The Westminster Confession of Faith is unparalleled in my estimation, but it is now largely
repudiated by the church that owned it for years. The Heidelberg Cate-
chism is a marvelous confession, but who is following it? Who believes these wonderful creeds in our day? The churches have a form of
godliness but are denying the power thereof. They have a name that
they live, but they are dead. They are neither hot nor cold—they are
lukewarm.

This is the condition of the church today, and unfortunately, it is
the condition of a great many so-called fundamental, conservative
churches. Thank God that there are many who do not come under this
classification. But the thing that is absolutely startling and frighten-
ing and fearful is that He says, "I will spue thee out of my mouth." In
other words, "I will vomit you out of my mouth." Does that sound to
you like the church which He's going to rapture, to whom He says, "I
go to prepare a place for you. And if I go and prepare a place for you, I
will come again, and receive you unto myself; that where I am, there
ye may be also" (John 14:2–3)? I don't think so. That is the church He
draws to Himself, but here is a church He just vomits out because it is
lukewarm. Lukewarm water makes you sick at your stomach. I am of

the opinion that if He spoke to a lot of churches today, He would say, "You make Me sick at My stomach. You're *professed* Christians. You say you love Me. You *say* it, but you don't mean it."

This is a heart-searching message for this hour because we are living in the time of the Laodicean church and of the Philadelphian church. Both of them are side by side, and there is a great bifurcation in Christianity today. It is not in denominations, and it is not Romanism and Protestantism. The great bifurcation consists of those who believe the Word of God and follow it, love it, obey it, and those who reject it. That is the line of division today.

> **Because thou sayest, I am rich, and increased with goods, and have need of nothing; and knowest not that thou art wretched, and miserable, and poor, and blind, and naked [Rev. 3:17].**

> *Thou sayest, I am rich, and have gotten riches, and have need of nothing; and thou dost not know that thou art the wretched one and miserable (the object of pity) and poor and blind and naked.*

"Because thou sayest, I am rich." The city of Laodicea was a rich city. I suppose that Laodicea and Sardis were probably two of the richest cities in that entire area at that particular time.

"Because thou sayest, I am rich, and increased with goods, and have need of nothing." They believed that the dollar was the answer to every problem of life. After World War II that was the assumption that the American government was run on. All we did was dole out dollars all over the world, thinking that we would buy friends, make peace, and settle the problems of the world. Very frankly, I believe that our nation has probably complicated the world more than anything else. We thought that all we had to do was to allocate money and we would solve the problems of the world. My friend, riches never solved any problem. This church in Laodicea tried it: "I am rich, and increased with goods, and have need of nothing; and knowest not that thou art wretched, and miserable, and poor, and blind, and naked."

The Laodicean church made its boast of material possessions. Conversely, the church in Smyrna was poor in material things. It was the church of slaves and poor folk. There were not many rich and not many noble in the early church. Paul writes in 1 Corinthians 1:26, "For ye see your calling, brethren, how that not many wise men after the flesh, not many mighty, not many noble, are called."

The present-day church boasts of large membership, prominent people, huge attendance, generous giving, and ornate buildings. A phenomenal growth in Protestant congregations, 242,000 in 1970 to 78,900,152 in 1980 (according to the *World Christian Encyclopedia*) would indicate the possibility of a church on fire for God. And there are other indications: Wealth beyond the wildest dreams of our forefathers; mass evangelistic meetings attended by tens of thousands; and use of other mass media such as radio and literature increasing constantly.

Worldly wealth is the measuring rod for the modern church. Spiritual values have been lost sight of or are entirely ignored. The church as a whole is not only rich in earthly goods, but also it actually is in the business of accumulating wealth. People are urged to make their wills in favor of so-called Christian organizations. Some radio and television programs and other professed Christian works are operated as promotional schemes to raise money to provide luxurious care for the promoters. My friend, you ought to check how the money you give to Christian work is being spent. When you write your will, I hope you will leave money for Christian work, but you ought to make sure that after you are gone, it is going to be spent for that which you intended.

On the spiritual side of the ledger, the Laodicean church is "the wretched one." It is worse off than any of the seven churches. It is to be pitied because it is spiritually poverty-stricken. In it is no study of the Word, no love of Christ, and no witnessing of His saving grace; yet it is blind to its own true condition. It lacks the covering of the robe of righteousness.

A pastor in Arlington, Virginia, put this in his church bulletin some years ago. It is an "Open Letter to Jane Ordinary"—

Dear Jane:

I am writing to help you shake this feeling of uselessness that has overtaken you. Several times you've said that you don't see how Christ can possibly use you. The church must bear part of the responsibility for making you feel as you do. I have in mind the success-story mentality of the church. Our church periodicals tell the story of John J. Moneybags who uses his influential position to witness for Christ. At the church youth banquet, we have a testimony from All-American football star, Ox Kickoffsky, who commands the respect of his teammates when he witnesses for Christ. We are led to think that if you don't have the leverage of stardom or a big position in the business world, you might as well keep your mouth shut. Nobody cares what Christ has done for you.

We've forgotten an elementary fact about Christian witness, something that should encourage you: God has chosen what the world calls foolish to shame the wise. He has chosen what the world calls weak to shame the strong. He has chosen things of little strength and of small repute, yes, and even things which have no real existence to explode the pretensions of the things that are, that no man may boast in the presence of God.

When Jesus Christ chose His disciples, He didn't choose Olympic champs or Roman senators. He chose simple people like you. Some were fishermen, one was a political extremist, another was a publican, a nobody in that society. But these men turned the Roman world upside down for Christ. How did they do it? Through their popularity? They had none. Their position? They had none. Their power was the power of Christ through the Holy Spirit.

Jane, don't forget that we still need the ordinary in the hands of Christ to turn the world upside down.

In the church today we sing:

The Church's one foundation is Jesus Christ her Lord;
She is His new creation by water and the word:

From heaven He came and sought her to be His holy bride;
With His own blood He bought her, and for her life He died.
"The Church's One Foundation"
—Samuel J. Stone

Yet the inscription on the cathedral in Lübeck, Germany, is still true:

Thus speaketh Christ our Lord to us:

Ye call Me Master and obey Me not.
Ye call Me Light and see Me not.
Ye call Me Way and walk Me not.
Ye call Me Life and choose Me not.
Ye call Me Wise and follow Me not.
Ye call Me Fair and love Me not.
Ye call Me Rich and ask Me not.
Ye call Me Eternal and seek Me not.
Ye call Me Noble and serve Me not.
Ye call Me Gracious and trust Me not.
Ye call Me Might and honor Me not.
Ye call Me Just and fear Me not.
If I condemn you, blame Me not.

This is the church in Laodicea. This is the church that Stanley High spoke of when he said:

The church has failed to tell me that I am a sinner. The church has failed to deal with me as a lost individual. The church has failed to offer me salvation in Jesus Christ alone. The church has failed to tell me of the horrible consequences of sin, the certainty of hell, and the fact that Jesus Christ alone can save. We need more of the last judgment and less of the Golden Rule, more of the living God and the living devil as well, more of a heaven to gain and a hell to shun. The church must bring me not a message of cultivation but of rebirth. I might fail that kind of church, but that kind of church will not fail me.

My friend, we are living in the Laodicean period today, and the church is failing to witness to the saving grace of God.

> **I counsel thee to buy of me gold tried in the fire, that thou mayest be rich; and white raiment, that thou mayest be clothed, and that the shame of thy nakedness do not appear; and anoint thine eyes with eye-salve, that thou mayest see [Rev. 3:18].**

"I counsel thee to buy of me gold tried in the fire, that thou mayest be rich"—this is the precious blood of Christ.

"And white raiment, that thou mayest be clothed, and that the shame of thy nakedness do not appear"—this speaks of the righteousness of Christ.

"And anoint thine eyes with eye-salve, that thou mayest see"—this speaks of the Holy Spirit who opens the eyes of believers today.

This admonition was very meaningful to the church at Laodicea. Sir William Ramsay has this very helpful comment in his excellent book, *The Letters to the Seven Churches of Asia:*

> The Laodicean Church must also learn that it is blind, but yet not incurably blind. It is suffering from disease, and needs medical treatment. But the physicians of its famous medical school can do nothing for it. The tabloids which they prescribe, and which are now used all over the civilized world, to reduce to powder and smear on the eyes, will be useless for this kind of ophthalmia. The Laodiceans must buy the tabloid from the Author himself, at the price of suffering and steadfastness.

> **As many as I love, I rebuke and chasten: be zealous therefore, and repent [Rev. 3:19].**

This word *zealous* means "to be hot." This is His last message to the church. He says, "Be zealous." Be hot. Get on fire for God. He is ordering this church to forsake its lukewarm state, and He says, "Repent." This church needs repentance more than all the others. And the message of repentance is for the contemporary church, but you will not be popular if you preach that, I can assure you. It is not too late even for those in this church to turn to Christ: "As many as I love, I rebuke and chasten: be zealous therefore, and repent."

Beginning at verse 20 is a general invitation which goes out from the Lord Jesus at any time—

> **Behold, I stand at the door, and knock: if any man hear my voice, and open the door, I will come in to him, and will sup with him, and he with me [Rev. 3:20].**

This is a picture of the Lord Jesus at the heart's door of the sinner. It is a glorious picture. The English artist, Holman Hunt, attempted to put this concept on canvas. He pictured Christ standing at a door. When he first painted the picture, he invited his artist friends to criticize. One of them said to him, "Holman, you have left off a very important part of the door. You left off the handle of the door." Hunt replied, "This door is a picture of the human heart, and the handle of the door is on the *inside*." This is the picture of Christ we have in Revelation. He stands at the door and knocks. He will not crash the door. Regardless of what some extremists say on this matter of election, the Lord Jesus has moved heaven and hell to get to the door of your heart, but when He gets there, He will stop and knock. You will have to open the door to let Him in.

"I will come in to him, and will sup with him, and he with me." This speaks of fellowship, of feeding on the Word of God, and of coming to know Jesus Christ better.

> **To him that overcometh will I grant to sit with me in my throne, even as I also overcame, and am set down with my Father in his throne [Rev. 3:21].**

Again, I call attention to the fact that when the Lord Jesus speaks of His relationship with the Father, He always makes it unique. He says, "My Father." He said, ". . . I ascend unto my Father . . ." (John 20:17, italics mine)—not our Father—because the relationship is always different with Him.

The Lord Jesus is preparing us for the next scene that will be coming up when He says, "and am set down with my Father in his throne." This is the picture that we are going to see in the chapters which follow.

He that hath an ear, let him hear what the Spirit saith unto the churches [Rev. 3:22].

This is a special message from the Lord Jesus to all the churches for which you need the blood-tipped ear to hear. This is the reason that you and I must be very careful in our study of the Word of God, that we not run ahead of the Spirit of God, but that we let Him be our teacher. If you have a blood-tipped ear, He wants you to hear what He has to say. Only the Spirit of God can make the Word of God real to you.

This concludes the messages to these seven churches. These are "the things which are," and they have been very important. I have spent a lot of time with these seven churches because they relate to the period in which we live and to our crowd. If we are a member of His church, we are also a member of His body, a part of that great company, beginning with the Day of Pentecost and coming down to the present hour, who have trusted the Lord Jesus as their Savior.

We have seen these seven churches blocked off into very definite periods of time, and they are largely fulfilled. I believe that we are in the period of the last two churches. As we have said before, there is a bifurcation in the organized, visible church today. There is that church, represented by the Laodicean church, which is moving farther and farther into the apostasy, and there is also that church which is staying by the Word of God, the church represented by the Philadelphian church. This is the church which will be raptured. The other church has a tremendous organization, including all the denominations, all those which profess to be Christian churches but which have long since departed from the Word of God and from the person of Christ. This is the division that exists in the church. One church will be raptured; the other will go into the Great Tribulation Period.

There has been a message for each of these churches. Personally, I enjoy going through these messages since I have now made several trips to the churches in Turkey, that is, Asia Minor. I have visited the ruins of all seven of these churches at least twice and some of them as many as four or five times. As we have come to each church, I can see the ruins before my eyes, and I can visualize the local situation. The Lord Jesus spoke to that local situation, and He was also blocking off all of church history because these are seven representative churches which cover the complete period of the church while it is here on the earth. And there is also a message in each of these for you and for me today.

To the church at Ephesus, there was a warning given that is also for us today. It was a warning of the danger of getting away from the best love, that is, getting away from a personal and loving relationship with Jesus Christ. The real test of any believer, especially those who are attempting to serve Him, is not your little method or mode or system or your dedication or any of the things that are so often emphasized today. The one question is: Do you love Him? Do you love the Lord Jesus? When you love Him, you will be in a right relationship with Him, but when you begin to depart from the person of Christ, it will finally lead to lukewarmness. The apostate church was guilty of lukewarmness. It may not seem to be too bad, but it is the worst condition that anyone can be in. A great preacher in upper New York state said: "Twenty lukewarm Christians hurt the cause of Christ more than one blatant atheist." A lukewarm church is a disgrace to Christ.

The Lord Jesus told the church in Smyrna not to fear suffering. Believe me, that is one thing that we in the church are frightened of today. We do not want to pay a price for serving the Lord Jesus, and yet that is His method.

To the church in Pergamum He said, "But I have a few things against thee, because thou hast there them that hold the doctrine of Balaam. . . . So hast thou also them that hold the doctrine of the Nicolaitans, which thing I hate" (Rev. 2:14–15). There is a grave danger in wrong doctrine today, and that was the thing that was wrong in the church in Pergamum.

To the church in Thyatira He said, "Notwithstanding I have a few things against thee, because thou sufferest that woman Jezebel, which calleth herself a prophetess, to teach and to seduce my servants to commit fornication, and to eat things sacrificed unto idols" (Rev. 2:20). The "new morality" is a grave danger for many today. Some folk think they can accept Christ and then live on a low plane. You will not get by with it, my friend, if you are His child.

In the church in Sardis, the Protestant church, there was the danger of spiritual deadness. He said, "I know thy works, that thou hast a name that thou livest, and art dead" (v. 1). What about your church, brother? Is it alive? Are you alive? Or are you dead in a dead church today? Many folk are in that condition, and yet they talk about holding the historic doctrines of the faith. But, my friend, the glaring defect in Protestantism today is deadness. And that is the worst thing of all.

The church in Philadelphia was not in any grave danger. The Lord Jesus does not condemn that church at all, but He does say, "Behold, I come quickly: hold that fast which thou hast, that no man take thy crown" (v. 11). What was it they had? He had commended them because they had kept His Word. We, too, need to be careful about this. As I look back now over the years of my ministry, I see men who started out true to the faith, many of them much stronger men than I was, men who defended the Word of God in a way that I did not in those early days, but they have now departed from the faith. I am amazed at that, but that is a grave danger even in the church in Philadelphia today. Nothing should deter us at all from keeping His Word.

To the church in Laodicea the Lord Jesus said, "So then because thou art lukewarm, and neither cold nor hot, I will spue thee out of my mouth" (v. 16). This is the apostate church which professes to be Christian but lacks reality. But even to this church He issues a final call to repentance and an invitation to come to Himself.

CHAPTER 4

THEME: The church in heaven with Christ

We have seen the history of the church in the seven churches of chapters 2—3, but as we come to chapter 4, the question naturally arises: What has happened to the church? From chapter 4 through the rest of the Book of Revelation, there is no mention of the church except when you get to the invitation at the end, which is a general invitation and hasn't anything to do with the chronology of the book. From here on you will not find the word church mentioned. Up to this point, the word church has occurred again and again, in fact nineteen times. But now the church goes off the air—there is no mention of it. It has gone off the air because it went up in the air; it was caught up in the air to meet the Lord in the air. The church has gone to heaven—that is what has happened to it. The Rapture takes place during the Philadelphian period, and the so-called church which continues on the earth is just an organization. It will go through the Great Tribulation Period, and we are finally going to hear it called a great harlot—what a frightful designation! Actually, the most frightful picture in the Bible is the seventeenth chapter of Revelation. Are we going to see the church again? Yes, but she is no longer a church; she is a bride—a bride adorned for her Husband.

Chapters 4—22 comprise the final major division of this very wonderful book. John was given the division of this book, and he passed it on to us. We ought not to miss it, for He said in chapter 1, verse 19, "Write the things which thou hast seen, and the things which are, and the things which shall be hereafter"—that is, meta tauta, meaning "after these things." "Things which must be hereafter" of verse 1 corresponds to "the things which shall be hereafter" of chapter 1, verse 19. Both are meta tauta in the Greek, indicating a change from this to an entirely different scene and subject.

Several striking facts make it self-evident that we advance to a new division beginning with chapter 4. The climate and conditions change radically:

1. The church is no longer seen in the world, although up to chapter 4, there have been nineteen references to the church in the world. In fact, the subject of chapters 2—3 has been entirely devoted to the church in the world. However, from chapter 4 to the end of the Revelation the church is never mentioned in connection with the world. The final and lone reference is a concluding testimony after the world's little day has ended (see Rev. 22:16). Christ said of His own, "They are not of the world, even as I am not of the world" (John 17:16). He also said to His own men, ". . . I will come again, and receive you unto myself; that where I am, there ye may be also" (John 14:3).

2. The scene definitely shifts to heaven in chapter 4. Since the church is still the subject, we follow it now to its new home—heaven. How did the church get to heaven? This is a good question, and Paul gives the answer: "Then we which are alive and remain shall be caught up together with them in the clouds, to meet the Lord in the air: and so shall we ever be with the Lord" (1 Thess. 4:17). He defines the operation in 1 Corinthians 15:51–52: "Behold, I shew you a mystery; we shall not all sleep, but we shall all be changed, in a moment, in the twinkling of an eye, at the last trump: for the trumpet shall sound, and the dead shall be raised incorruptible, and we shall be changed."

Faith places the sinner on the launching pad, in the guided missile of the church, from whence he shall go to meet the Lord in the air. The saints enter the opened door to heaven. The church is with Christ, and Christ is in heaven, directing the events of the Great Tribulation Period that we are going to see when we get to chapter 6.

3. The church is not a name but a definition of those who have trusted Christ in this age. This is something which we need to get fixed in our minds because our thinking on this today is often muddled. The word church is ekklesia in the Greek; kaleō means "to call," and ek means "out of." Therefore, ekklesia means "a group of people called out of the world."

When the church arrives at its destination in heaven, it loses the name by which it was known in the world and other terms are used to describe it. We are going to see it in chapter 4 as twenty-four elders, representatives of the church in heaven. We are also going to see the church in heaven as a bride, coming down to her new home, the New Jerusalem.

The apostate organization, which bears the ecclesiastical terminology and continues on in the world, is not hereafter given the title of "church" either, but the frightful label of "the harlot." The late Dr. George Gill said years ago in a seminary class, "There are going to be some churches which will meet the next Sunday after the Rapture, and they won't be missing a member—they will all be there." Why? Because it is the church of Laodicea—that is, it professes to be Christian but lacks reality.

4. The judgments beginning at chapter 6 would not be in harmony with the gracious provision and promise that God has made to the church. If the church remained in the world, it would frustrate the grace of God because He has promised to deliver us from judgment.

5. Finally, to continue from chapter 3 to chapter 4 without recognizing the break is to ignore the normal and natural division in the book as stated in chapter 1, verse 19.

As we enter this last division of the book with all of its judgment and wrath, it is well to keep in our perspective that Jesus Christ is central. He is directing all events as He brings them to a successful but determined conclusion. There is "in the midst of the throne . . . a Lamb" (Rev. 7:17). He is a Lamb because He died for the sins of the world. And He is the One who is going to judge.

After these things, after the church things have concluded, the scene shifts from earth to heaven. It is a radical change. However, the Word of God describes personages and activities in heaven as normally as it described them on earth. There is no strain or involvement in superstition or mystery. The bridge over the great gulf is passed with ease and a reverent restraint. Only the Holy Spirit could describe things in heaven with as much ease as He describes things on the earth. What would have happened if a man had written this book? You know that the minute he got to the heavenly scene, he would have the wildest sort of things to say. How do I know that? Well, read the books that are out today which try to describe the overworld and the underworld and the unseen world. They are always rather startling and amazing. In fact, the use of this approach is one way that we can know a book is false. There is an awful obsession today, even among some Christians, with the subject of demons and of the Devil. I have no truck with that outfit at all. I have often been asked why I haven't written a book on this subject. Frankly, at first I thought I would, but when so many books started coming out, all as wild as a March Hare and all dealing with the sensational, I changed my mind. You don't have the sensational here in Revelation. We simply move to heaven, and the scene is awe inspiring, but it lacks that which man would put in.

The church is not seen under the familiar name it had in the world, but is now the priesthood of believers with the Great High Priest. Heavenly scenes and creatures greet us in this section (chs. 4—5) before our attention is drawn to the earth where, at the opening of the Great Tribulation, the four horsemen are to ride.

THE THRONE OF GOD

Christ is viewed here in His threefold office of Prophet, Priest, and King. He is worshiped as God because He is God.

After this I looked, and, behold, a door was opened in heaven: and the first voice which I heard was as it were of a trumpet talking with me; which said, Come up hither, and I will shew thee things which must be hereafter [Rev. 4:1].

Here is my translation of this first verse:

After these things [Gr.: meta tauta] I saw, and behold a door set open in heaven; and the first voice which I heard, a voice as of a trumpet speaking with me and saying, Come up hither, and I will show thee the things which must come to pass after these things [meta tauta].

"After these things" *(meta tauta)* is used twice here; it both opens and closes the verse. This repetition certainly lends great emphasis and importance to the phrase. Apparently, John was afraid the amillennialists would miss it; so he used it twice in this particular place.

"I saw"—that is the eye-gate. "I heard"—that is the ear-gate. This is like a television program which we are looking at. This is the first great television program. We have had a wonderful treat in our day to view a television program from the moon, but that is nothing in comparison—here is a television program from heaven! This ought to interest believers a great deal and not cause us to take off like a sky-rocket into some wild sort of dreamy stuff. Heaven is a real place. There is a lot of reality there, and we ought not to get uptight over this scene that is now before us. We need to handle it in a normal way, but I admit that I cannot help but get excited about it all.

"I saw, and behold a door set open in heaven." This is one of the four open doors in the Book of Revelation:

1. In chapter 3, verse 8, speaking to the church in Philadelphia, the Lord Jesus says, "I have set before thee an open door." It seems that this refers to a door of opportunity for giving out the Word of God.

2. The open door of invitation and identification with Christ is in chapter 3, verse 20: "Behold, I stand at the door, and knock: if any man hear my voice, and open the door, I will come in to him, and will sup with him, and he with me." That door is the door to your heart.

3. We have an open door here in verse 1, which is the way to God through Christ, as we shall see.

4. In chapter 19, verse 11, we see a door opened in heaven again. That is the open door through which Christ will come at His second coming. He comes out at the end of the Great Tribulation to put down all of the unrighteousness and rebellion against God and to establish His kingdom.

John did not see this door opening as the Authorized Version of verse 1 suggests. This door was open all the time. It is the door through which believers have come to God for over nineteen hundred years. "Jesus saith unto him, I am the way, the truth, and the life: no man cometh unto the Father, but by me" (John 14:6). He also said, "I am the door: by me if any man enter in, he shall be saved, and shall go in and out, and find pasture" (John 10:9). The open door to heaven is the Lord Jesus Christ. He also is the One who will come to the door of your heart—that is the wonder and glory of it all.

We enter by faith. In modern terminology, we might express it thus: faith puts us on the launching pad of the church, which is Christ, and at the Rapture we go through this door like a guided missile. It is not just shot out into space going nowhere, but if man can hit the target of the moon, I do not think the Lord Jesus will have any trouble getting His church into heaven.

"Come up hither" is heaven's invitation to John, and it is an invitation to all of the fellowship that know Christ as Savior. John wrote in 1 John 1:3: "That which we have seen and heard declare we unto you, that ye also may have fellowship with us: and truly our fellowship is with the Father, and with his Son Jesus Christ."

John is saying in effect, "We heard it, we saw it, and we declare it unto you. I am letting you know this so that you can have fellowship also, and one of these days you will be going up through that open door."

"And the first voice which I heard, a voice as of a trumpet speaking with me." This is the sound which calls the church to meet Christ in the air. And whose voice is it? It is the voice of Christ. This introduces us to one of the simple symbols which occurs frequently from here on in the Revelation. That it is a symbol is evident—a trumpet does not speak. Jazz devotees describe the trumpet playing of certain musicians by saying that their trumpets "talk." When jazz addicts say that, they are just using a symbol. A trumpet never talks. The voice of Christ is like a trumpet, and this is the voice that Paul wrote of in 1 Thessalonians 4:16–17: "For the Lord himself shall descend from heaven with a shout, with the voice of the archangel, and with the trump of God: and the dead in Christ shall rise first: then we which are alive and remain shall be caught up together with them in the clouds, to meet the Lord in the air, and so shall we ever be with the Lord."

This is a definite statement concerning the Rapture. When anyone tells you that the word rapture is not in the Bible, remember that the

Greek word for "caught up" is *harpazō*; it means "caught up, raptured, or snatched up." Hal Lindsey calls the Rapture "the great snatch." I guess that is good vocabulary for young people today, but I prefer the term "caught up," and it means rapture. If you don't like the word *rapture*, then call it *harpazō*. That's what Paul called it. We are to be caught up, and His voice will be like a trumpet. It pulled John up, and someday it will pull you and me up.

"Come up hither, and I will shew thee the things which must come to pass after these things." After what things? After the church has completed its earthly run and is caught up.

> **And immediately I was in the spirit; and, behold, a throne was set in heaven, and one sat on the throne [Rev. 4:2].**
>
> *At once (straightway) I found myself in the Spirit: and behold, a throne set in heaven, and one sitting on the throne.*

"At once (straightway)" denotes the brevity of time, which is one of the characteristics of the Rapture. Paul said that we are to be caught up "in a moment, in the twinkling of an eye" (see 1 Cor. 15:51–52). A twinkling of an eye is pretty brief. Some psychologist has measured it. He considered the twinkling of an eye to be, not the going down of the eyelid, but the going up of the eyelid—that is reducing it to a fine point! But he determined that it is 1/1000 of a second. That is how quick the Rapture is going to be—immediately, straightway, at once.

"I found myself in the Spirit." In other words, the Holy Spirit is still guiding John into new truth and is showing him things to come (see John 16:13).

"And, behold, a throne set in heaven, and one sitting on the throne." The throne was already there, but John now sees it for the first time. Our attention is now directed to the center of attraction. The throne represents the universal sovereignty and rulership of God. It means that He is in control. The general headquarters of this universe is in heaven, not in Washington, D.C., or London or Moscow or any

other place down here. This is the picture that we are given in the
Word of God. We read in Psalm 11:4, "The LORD is in his holy temple,
the LORD's throne is in heaven: his eyes behold, his eyelids try, the
children of men" (see also Ps. 47:8; 97:2; 103:19; Ezek. 1:26–28). It is
the throne of God the Father, and Jesus sits at His right hand. Psalm
110:1 tells us, "The LORD said unto my Lord, Sit thou at my right
hand, until I make thine enemies thy footstool" (see also Heb. 1:3;
12:2). The Lord Jesus is in charge of all events here.

The throne of grace now becomes a throne of judgment. This is
another reason that I say very definitely that the church is gone from
the world when this takes place. If the church were still on the earth
when Christ has left the place of intercession and has come to the
place of judgment, He is in the wrong place for the church.

**And he that sat was to look upon like a jasper and a
sardine stone: and there was a rainbow round about the
throne, in sight like unto an emerald [Rev. 4:3].**

All that we see here is color, beautiful color like precious stones. We
do not get a picture of God at all—He never has been photographed.
Our attention is directed to the One who is seated on the throne. Although He is God the Father, we should understand this to be the
throne of the triune God. Nevertheless, the three persons of the Trinity
are distinguished: (1) God the Holy Spirit in verses 2 and 5; (2) God
the Father here in verse 3; and (3) God the Son in verse 5 of chapter 5.
What we have before us here is the Trinity upon the throne.

John could distinguish no form of a person on the throne, only the
brilliance and brightness of precious stones.

"And he that sat was to look upon like a jasper." The jasper stone
was the last stone identified in the breastplate of the high priest (see
Exod. 28:20). It was first in the foundation of the New Jerusalem and
also the first seen in the wall of the New Jerusalem (see Rev. 21:18–
19). It was a many-colored stone with purple predominating. Some
identify it with a diamond. It was in the breastplate of the high priest
of Israel, representing little Benjamin whom Jacob called "the son of

my right hand" Perhaps this speaks of Christ as He ascended and took His place at the right hand of the Father.

The "sardine stone" is the sixth stone in the foundation of the New Jerusalem (see Rev. 21:20). Pliny says it was discovered in Sardis from which it derived its name. In color it was a fiery red. The sardine stone was the first stone in the breastplate of the high priest, representing the tribe of Reuben, the firstborn of Jacob. And Christ is the Son of God, the firstborn from the dead.

"Rainbow" is the Greek word iris, which can also mean "halo." While the rainbow is polychrome, here it is emerald, which is green (see Ezek. 1:28). After the judgment of the Flood, the rainbow appeared as a reminder of God's covenant not to destroy the earth again with a flood (see Gen. 9:13–15). It appears here before the judgment of the Great Tribulation as a reminder that a flood will not be used in judgment. Green is the color of the earth. The suggestion here is that of the prophet Habakkuk: ". . . in wrath remember mercy" (Hab. 3:2)—and God will do that.

THE TWENTY-FOUR ELDERS

And round about the throne were four and twenty seats: and upon the seats I saw four and twenty elders sitting, clothed in white raiment; and they had on their heads crowns of gold [Rev. 4:4].

There has been a great deal of speculation as to who these elders are. The Greek word for "elders" is presbuteros. By the way, the word presbyterian comes from that, and I am reminded of the story about the little girl who came home from her Presbyterian Sunday school, and her mother asked her what they had talked about. "We talked about heaven," the little girl replied. "Well, what did they say about it?" her mother asked. "The teacher said that there were only twenty-four Presbyterians there!"

Seriously, elders were representatives. We know that Israel had elders and that elders were appointed in the early churches to rule and to represent the entire church (see Titus 1:5). Their role was clearly understood by the people in John's day. These twenty-four elders stand for the total church from Pentecost to the Rapture. Therefore, I can say categorically and dogmatically that here is the church in heaven.

"White raiment" is the righteousness of Christ (see 2 Cor. 5:21).

"Crowns of gold" indicates that the church will rule with Christ (see 1 Cor. 6:3). Crowns are also given as rewards (see 2 Tim. 4:8; James 1:12; 1 Pet. 5:4) when the *bema* judgment, the judgment seat of Christ, takes place.

> And out of the throne proceeded lightnings and thunderings and voices: and there were seven lamps of fire burning before the throne, which are the seven Spirits of God [Rev. 4:5].

The tense here is the present tense; it should be *proceed*, not *proceeded*. It is taking place right there and then.

"Lightnings and thunderings" always precede a storm in the Midwest and generally indicate the intensity of the storm. I think that the meaning here is that judgment is coming.

"And voices" indicates that it is not a haphazard judgment, but it is directed by the One on the throne.

"The seven Spirits of God" is a clear reference to the Holy Spirit.

THE FOUR LIVING CREATURES

> And before the throne there was a sea of glass like unto crystal: and in the midst of the throne, and round about the throne, were four beasts full of eyes before and behind [Rev. 4:6].

"A sea of glass" denotes its appearance and not the material of which it is made. This sea is before the throne of God and is another indication that the emphasis is not on mercy but on judgment. This sea represents the holiness and righteousness of God (see Matt. 5:8; Heb. 12:14).

We are told in 1 Thessalonians 3:13, "To the end he may stablish your hearts unblameable in holiness before God, even our Father, at the coming of our Lord Jesus Christ with all his saints." This placid sea indicates the position of rest to which the church has come. No longer is she the victim of the storms of life. No longer is she out there on the tossing sea.

"Four beasts" are literally "four living creatures." The Greek word is zōa, from which we get our English word zoo. It doesn't mean a wild beast as we might think. We will have a wild beast when we get to chapter 13, but that is a different word and a different type of beast. This is just a living creature. The emphasis is not upon the bestial, but upon the vital, upon the fact that they are living.

"Four beasts full of eyes before and behind." This speaks of their alertness and awareness. They resemble both the cherubim of Ezekiel 1:5–10; 10:20; and the seraphim of Isaiah 6:2–3.

> **And the first beast was like a lion, and the second beast like a calf, and the third beast had a face as a man, and the fourth beast was like a flying eagle [Rev. 4:7].**

I agree with those who identify each of these living creatures with the Gospel which it represents, and I believe this is accurate, although such an application is questioned a great deal.

"The first living creature was like a lion," and the first Gospel represents the Lord Jesus as the King. He was born a King, He lived a King, He died a King, He was raised a King, and He is coming again as a King. Everything He does in the Gospel of Matthew He does as the King. Remember that God said that the tribe of Judah was like a lion, that the King, the Ruler, would come from that tribe, and that the scepter would not depart from Judah until Shiloh came (see Gen. 49:9–10; Rev. 5:5).

"The second living creature like a calf [ox]." This is the beast of burden, the servant animal domesticated. In the Gospel of Mark,

Christ is presented as the Servant. There is no genealogy given in this Gospel. If you hire someone to mow your lawn or to wash your dishes, you do not ask him who his papa and mama are. What difference does it make? You want to know whether or not he can do the job. The Gospel of Mark presents Christ as the Servant.

"The third living creature had a face as a man." The third Gospel, the Gospel of Luke, presents the Lord Jesus as the Son of Man. It is His humanity that is emphasized.

"The fourth living creature was like a flying eagle." He communicates the deity of Christ as seen in the Gospel of John.

These living creatures also represent the animal world, as suggested by Godet. The lion represents wild beasts, the calf represents domesticated beasts, the eagle represents birds, and man is the head of all creation. Note that there is no mention of fish. In the new heaven and the new earth, there will be no more sea, and since there is no sea, you will not need any fish. Nor will there be reptiles. The serpent will not be there to introduce sin as he did at the beginning.

> And the four beasts had each of them six wings about him; and they were full of eyes within: and they rest not day and night, saying, Holy, holy, holy, Lord God Almighty, which was, and is, and is to come [Rev. 4:8].

These six wings correspond to the seraphim of Isaiah 6:2.

Instead of *had*, it should be *having*—this is the present tense. This is where the action is, and this is taking place.

That which they say repeatedly is, "Holy, holy, holy, Lord God Almighty." This is the same refrain as that of the seraphim in Isaiah 6:3.

"Which was, and is, and is to come" refers to Christ. He identified Himself at the very beginning of this book in just that way: "I am Alpha and Omega, the beginning and the ending, saith the Lord, which is, and which was, and which is to come, the Almighty" (Rev. 1:8). He is identified for us, and therefore we do not need to speculate in places like this.

> And when those beasts give glory and honour and
> thanks to him that sat on the throne, who liveth for ever
> and ever,
>
> The four and twenty elders fall down before him that sat
> on the throne, and worship him that liveth for ever and
> ever, and cast their crowns before the throne, saying,
>
> Thou art worthy, O Lord, to receive glory and honour
> and power: for thou hast created all things, and for thy
> pleasure they are and were created [Rev. 4:9–11].

This is the first great worship scene which we see in heaven.

When should be whensoever, indicating that this is a continual act of worship. In other words, praise and adoration are the eternal activity of God's creatures in heaven. The creature worships the Creator as the triune God: "Holy, holy, holy." Worship is the activity of heaven.

I have a sermon which I have not preached in quite some while, which is entitled, "Why Do You Want to Go to Heaven?" Many people say that not everybody who is talking about heaven is going to heaven. The better question is, Why do you want to go to heaven? Is the idea to miss hell? I myself do not think that to be an unworthy motive, but may I say to you that if you go to heaven, you are going to find yourself either getting down on your face or getting up, worshiping the triune God and especially the Lord Jesus Christ. If you find worship boring down here and you are not interested in worshiping the Lord Jesus and expressing your heart's desire to Him, why in the world do you want to go to heaven? We are going to spend a lot of time up there worshiping Him.

"And cast their crowns before the throne." The crowns of the church are laid at Jesus' feet as an act of submission and worship. Many people talk of there being a crown for them over there. Frankly, if we get a crown at all, I think that after we wear it for awhile and the newness wears off, we are going to feel embarrassed. What in the world are we doing wearing a crown? The only One worthy up there is the Lord Jesus. Therefore, we are going to lay our crown at His feet.

"For thou hast created all things." Dr. Walvoord, in his very excellent book, *The Revelation of Jesus Christ*, calls attention to something here that I think is important. The living creatures give glory and honor and thanks to Him who sits on the throne. They worship Him for His attributes, because He is who He is. However, the four and twenty elders who represent the church worship Him not only because of His attributes, but also because of what He has done. Here they worship Him as Creator—"thou hast created all things, and for thy pleasure they are and were created." In other words, the church comes out of this little earth which is God's creation, and they join in the worship because He created this earth down here. Genesis 1:1 is accurate, and the church believes it.

"And for thy pleasure they are and were created." "For thy pleasure" is more accurately translated "because of thy will." The reason that God created this earth and that things are as they are is because it was in His plan and purpose. I do not understand a great deal of what He is doing, and I do not understand a great deal about this universe in which I live, but I do know that it is created this way because this is the way He wanted it. He is in charge, and we are to worship Him because He created this little earth. I am glad that He did, and I am glad that He created me. He could have forgotten all about me, but I am glad that I was in the plan and purpose of God. We worship Him because of that.

CHAPTER 5

THEME: The church in heaven with Christ—continued

Chapter 5 continues this scene of the church in heaven with Christ. I think it is well for us to spend a little time here to get acquainted with where we are going. I am sure that you would not buy real estate in Florida without seeing it first, although I had an uncle who did just that. After he went down and saw it, he reported that he had some of the finest alligators that he had ever seen—all of his property was under water! He had bought it sight unseen. We have a lot of uninhabitable desert here in California, and even in the Hawaiian Islands there are great areas of nothing but a lava bed. You had better know what you are buying. Therefore, if you are going to heaven, you will want to know something about where you are going, and that is the reason this chapter ought to be interesting to you.

In chapters 4—5 we find that the church (the body of believers) is in heaven with Christ. The Lord Jesus said to his disciples, "... I go to prepare a place for you. ... that where I am, there ye may be also" (John 14:2–3). We are going to be with Him.

The scene of chapter 5 is set in heaven, preparatory to the events of the Great Tribulation. Since the church is in heaven with Him, it surely could not go through the Great Tribulation down here on the earth. The throne was the center of chapter 4. The Lion and the Lamb, both of whom represent Christ, are the center of chapter 5. Christ is the Lamb on the throne. He is both Sovereign and Savior. He is in full charge of all the events which follow in this book. Let us not lose sight of Him.

THE BOOK WITH SEVEN SEALS

This chapter opens with *and*, a connective, a little conjunction, which indicates that something went before. It is the string that ties us back to chapter 4. Actually, we don't need a chapter division here because it is all the same subject.

> **And I saw in the right hand of him that sat on the throne a book written within and on the backside, sealed with seven seals [Rev. 5:1].**

Here is my translation of this verse:

> *And I saw on the right hand of Him that sat on the throne a book written within and on the back, close sealed (sealed tightly) with seven seals.*

"I saw"—John is the witness of these events; this is something that he sees. Someone pointed out to me in a letter sometime ago that I have the habit of saying, "Isn't this a wonderful picture?" or, "Isn't that a picture for you?" I wasn't aware that I use that expression as I teach, but I guess I do. I think that we ought to bring all our senses to bear upon the Word of God and especially in studying Revelation. John is *seeing*, and he is *hearing*. This is the reason that I frequently use slides to illustrate my sermons. I receive some criticism for that, but may I say to you, we need to see and hear a lot of things to aid our understanding of the Scriptures. The Word of God should grasp and lay hold of all of our senses, even of our taste and smell. For example, there are certain scenes in Revelation where you can smell the fire and brimstone.

God the Father holds here in His hand a scroll which is rolled tightly and sealed closely with seven seals. Stauffer is the one who calls our attention to the fact that the Roman law required that a will be sealed seven times, as illustrated in the wills left by Augustus and Vespasian. While it is interesting that this method was used, we know that in the Book of Revelation the number seven is not just an accidental number and that it wasn't used only because they used it in the Roman Empire.

Godet considers this scroll to be "the book of the new covenant." Others label it "the book of judgment." Walter Scott considered it "the revelation of God's purpose and counsel concerning the world." It perhaps should bear no title because it is, as Dr. Harry Ironside has suggested, the title deed to this world. You will remember that when the children of Israel were going into captivity, Jeremiah was instructed to have his servant go and buy some property and to get the title deed to it, because God promised that Israel was going to be returned to the land (see Jer. 32:6–15).

Who holds the title deed to this earth down here? It is none other than the Lord Jesus; He alone has it. In Daniel 7:13–14 we read: "I saw in the night visions, and, behold, one like the Son of man came with the clouds of heaven, and came to the Ancient of days, and they brought him near before him. And there was given him dominion, and glory, and a kingdom, that all people, nations, and languages, should serve him: his dominion is an everlasting dominion, which shall not pass away, and his kingdom that which shall not be destroyed."

This suggests, I believe, that what is being handed over to the Lord Jesus (we will see it handed over to Him) is the title deed to this world in which you and I live. He created it, He redeemed it, and it belongs to Him.

In Zechariah, which is a book that you need to know in order to know Revelation, we read: "Then I turned, and lifted up mine eyes, and looked, and behold a flying roll. And he said unto me, What seest thou? And I answered, I see a flying roll; the length thereof is twenty cubits, and the breadth thereof is ten cubits. Then said he unto me, This is the curse that goeth forth over the face of the whole earth: for every one that stealeth shall be cut off as on this side according to it; and every one that sweareth shall be cut off as on that side according to it" (Zech. 5:1–3).

This flying roll is the same thing as the scroll here in Revelation. Some think that the Ten Commandments are on this roll and that the world is to be judged by those commandments. I am not sure that that is it. Many suggestions have been made in an attempt to identify this book, but this is one place where we cannot be dogmatic.

The suggestion, which I consider to be more in line than any other, is that this book represents God's new covenant with Israel. God talks about this covenant a great deal. In Jeremiah we read, "Behold, the days come, saith the LORD, that I will make a new covenant with the house of Israel, and with the house of Judah. . . . I will put my law in their inward parts, and write it in their hearts; and will be their God, and they shall be my people" (Jer. 31:31, 33). Paul writes in Romans: "And so all Israel shall be saved: as it is written, There shall come out of Sion the Deliverer, and shall turn away ungodliness from Jacob: For this is my covenant unto them, when I shall take away their sins" (Rom. 11:26–27).

In Hebrews we find these words: "This is the covenant that I will make with them after those days, saith the Lord, I will put my laws into their hearts, and in their minds will I write them" (Heb. 10:16). This is what Jeremiah had spoken of. The writer to the Hebrews continues: "And their sins and iniquities will I remember no more. Now where remission of these is, there is no more offering for sin" (Heb. 10:17–18).

The old covenant which God had made with Israel depended upon man. The Ten Commandments said, "Don't, don't, don't." It depended upon the weak arm of the flesh, and as a result, it failed. This was not because there was anything wrong with the Ten Commandments or with the Law that God gave. The problem was with man. The same thing occurred in the Garden of Eden. Many people think that there was something wrong with the forbidden fruit or that the tree was something unusual. I think it was good fruit and just like any other. The problem was not the fruit on the tree but the pear (pair) on the ground! This New Covenant depends upon the power of the throne of God; it depends upon the Lord Jesus Christ.

> And I saw a strong angel proclaiming with a loud voice, Who is worthy to open the book, and to loose the seals thereof? [Rev. 5:2].

Who has the right and title to this world? Who can rule it? Who can establish justice and righteousness? Do you think that maybe the Democrats can do it? Do you think that the Republicans can do it? Do you think that any administration can do it? Do you think the United

Nations can do it? I trust that you are not so deluded at this late time in the history of the world that you believe that man can solve his own problems. The Word of God makes it very clear that he cannot.

"A strong angel" means a powerful angel. He has "a loud voice." This is speaking now of power, that which is needed to make this covenant effective.

> **And no man in heaven, nor in earth, neither under the earth, was able to open the book, neither to look thereon [Rev. 5:3].**

No man of Adam's line has a right to open the book and to take charge of this earth. There have been a great many who have tried to do it. Adam lost dominion through sin. Moses was the lawgiver, but he was also a lawbreaker. David and his line failed. None of Adam's line qualifies. There is none today. The Ruler must be a Redeemer, the Sovereign must be a Savior of mankind, and Jesus Christ is the only One. Stand aside, Adam, you cannot do it, and neither can any of your children. Satan is working at it, but he cannot do it either. The question is: Who is going to be able to do it?

> **And I wept much, because no man was found worthy to open and to read the book, neither to look thereon [Rev. 5:4].**

John is disturbed by this a great deal. This man had a real passion for prophecy. He had a holy affection and a pious curiosity. He wanted to look into the things that even angels cannot look into. John enters into the drama because he has come from earth. The Revelation was written in tears. Is the earth to continue in sin and sorrow? Is there no future for the earth? Listen to what Paul has to say: "And not only they, but ourselves also, which have the first-fruits of the Spirit, even we ourselves groan within ourselves, waiting for the adoption, to wit, the redemption of our body" (Rom. 8:23).

Is no one competent to rule this earth? John is overwhelmed by the possibility that there may be no one. Again Paul writes· "For we know that the whole creation groaneth and travaileth in pain together until now" (Rom. 8:22).

Personally, I believe that evolution is the most pessimistic philosophy and theory that anyone can entertain today. No wonder it has led to so many suicides among the intelligentsia. What hope is there for the future if it took millions of years to get to where we are today? Isn't there someone who can straighten out this problem? It is so petty and little and narrow-minded for politicians to say that they are going to make peace in our time. It is even more tragic to hear the church say that they can straighten out the affairs of the world or even that they can evangelize the world. My brother, may I say to you, there are just not any around who can qualify to open this book and to take charge of this earth that we are on. And John weeps a great deal because of this.

It is a good thing that this book was not opened here in Southern California because we have a whole passel of preachers who say that they can tell you what is on the inside of this book, on the outside, and all around it. They can even tell you what's on the cover! They have all the answers. If John had just been in California, instead of being on the island of Patmos, they could have given him the answers! Well, John didn't have the answer, but there will be One who can open the book, as we shall see.

CHRIST, THE LION AND THE LAMB

And one of the elders saith unto me, Weep not: behold, the Lion of the tribe of Juda, the Root of David, hath prevailed to open the book, and to loose the seven seals thereof [Rev. 5:5].

And one from among the elders saith unto me, Weep not: behold, the Lion of the tribe of Juda, the Root of David, hath overcome to open the book, and the seven seals thereof.

Evidently, any one of the elders could have answered. They had spiritual illumination. I think that this further identifies them as the

church because the Lord Jesus had said to His own: "Henceforth I call
you not servants; for the servant knoweth not what his lord doeth: but
I have called you friends; for all things that I have heard of my Father I
have made known unto you" (John 15:15).

The Lord Jesus Christ is the only One who has the right and title to
this earth. He not only redeemed you and me, but He also redeemed
the earth. He is identified in this section in all His ministries that
relate to the earth.

"The Lion of the tribe of Juda" identifies Him, of course, with
the tribe of Judah of the people of Israel. When old Jacob was dying,
he called his twelve sons around him, and this is the prophecy he
gave concerning Judah: "Judah is a lion's whelp: from the prey, my
son, thou art gone up: he stooped down, he couched as a lion, and as
an old lion; who shall rouse him up? The sceptre shall not depart
from Judah, nor a lawgiver from between his feet, until Shiloh come;
and unto him shall the gathering of the people be" (Gen. 49:9–10).
The Lord Jesus is the Lion of the tribe of Judah. He is also "the Root of
David." In 2 Samuel 7, that great chapter of God's covenant with
David, He says, "I am going to bring One in your line who shall rule,
not only over these people, but over the whole earth." The Lord Jesus
Christ has the right to rule, as He is the fulfillment of the prophecies
made in the Old Testament relative to the future of the world. All of
those prophecies will be fulfilled at His second coming to the earth to
establish His kingdom.

> And I beheld, and, lo, in the midst of the throne and of
> the four beasts, and in the midst of the elders, stood a
> Lamb as it had been slain, having seven horns and seven
> eyes, which are the seven Spirits of God sent forth into
> all the earth [Rev. 5:6].

John is still a spectator to this scene. He says, "I beheld, I saw this."

"A Lamb"—the word there is in the diminutive; literally, it means
a little lamb. This denotes its gentleness and its willingness to be sacrificed. Christ was led as a lamb to the slaughter, and He did not open

His mouth at all (see Isa. 53:7). He was the Lamb of God who taketh away the sin of the world (see John 1:29).

"As it had been slain" indicates the redemptive and vicarious, substitutionary death of Christ. The emphasis is upon the fact that He was slain with violence.

"Stood" should rather be "standing." This speaks of His resurrection. He is no longer seated at the right hand of God. He is moving now, and He is moving to power. He is coming to this earth. The judgment of the Tribulation is about to strike the earth. The winds are already blowing on the earth.

"In the midst of the throne" is indicative of the fact that He is before the throne and ready to act as the righteous Judge.

"Seven horns" denotes complete power. A horn speaks of power (see Dan. 7—8). He is omnipotent. "Seven eyes" denotes complete knowledge. Christ is omniscient. He is the omnipotent and omniscient God. He moves in the fullness of the Spirit, who is the Spirit of wisdom and understanding.

The Lord Jesus Christ is a Lion and a Lamb. The lion character refers to His second coming; the lamb character refers to His first coming. The lion is symbolic of His majesty; the lamb is symbolic of His meekness. As a lion He is a Sovereign; as a lamb He is a Savior. As a lion He is a Judge; as a lamb He is judged. The lion represents the government of God; the lamb represents the grace of God.

> And he came and took the book out of the right hand of
> him that sat upon the throne [Rev. 5:7].

"Took" is correctly "hath taken." The Lord Jesus moves to the throne through the Tribulation Period. He *judges* the world in righteousness before He reigns in righteousness. He is no longer the intercessor of the church, for the church is now with Him. He is beginning to act as Judge. The movement here is important.

> And when he had taken the book, the four beasts and
> four and twenty elders fell down before the Lamb, hav-

ing every one of them harps, and golden vials full of odours, which are the prayers of saints [Rev. 5:8].

"When he had taken [took] the book" is in the aorist tense, meaning completed action. This is the great movement of all creation, and the Lord Jesus takes over now.

Notice the worship of the Lamb by the four living creatures and the twenty-four elders. "Harps" denote praise. The elders do not play on the harps; they are just a token of praise to God. I am so glad to have found out that I am not going to be an angel playing on a harp in heaven—that just doesn't appeal to me! You may want a harp, and if you want one, I guess in heaven they will get one for you, but I am thankful that I don't have to have one.

The twenty-four elders act as priests. Only the church is a priesthood of believers in heaven. Dr. Carl Armerding gives the arresting thought that the prayer of Christ for believers in John 17 is answered in the elders: our Lord's prayer that they might know Him, that they might be with Him, and that they might behold His glory is all answered in this scene of the elders in heaven.

The "vials full of odours" is more accurately "bowls full of incense." These are identified as "the prayers of saints." Obviously, the elders represent the body of Christ, which is called the church and they are the priesthood.

> **And they sung a new song, saying, Thou art worthy to take the book, and to open the seals thereof: for thou wast slain, and hast redeemed us to God by thy blood out of every kindred, and tongue, and people, and nation;**
>
> **And hast made us unto our God kings and priests: and we shall reign on the earth [Rev. 5:9-10].**
>
> *And they sing a new song, saying, Worthy art thou to take the book and to open the seals of it: for thou wast slain and didst purchase unto God in thy blood [men] of every*

*tribe, tongue, people, and nation, and madest them unto
our God a kingdom and priests, and they shall reign on
the earth.*

"They" indicates that both the living creatures and the elders sing this
song. The angelic hosts join the church in praise.

"Sing" (present tense) denotes the continuation of praise. Praise is
directed to the Lamb with the book. He is praised now as the Redeemer of men in all ages and races. In heaven is going to be the first
time that I will sing. I have never been able to sing, but I am going to
be in that chorus, and I am going to sing praises unto Him.

The "new song" is the song of redemption. The old song is the
song of creation. In the Book of Job we are told that the sons of God
sang. They were singing because God was the Creator; they didn't
really know anything about the love of God then. Now we can sing
about our Savior who loves us and who gave Himself for us. What a
picture we have here!

"Worthy" reveals that He now fills the entire horizon of praise and
worship. Actually, worship is returning to *worth*, that which belongs
to Him; and He is the only One worthy of praise.

"And hast redeemed us to God by thy blood." They sing of His
shed blood in heaven. Down here many denominational churches are
taking out of their hymn books all references to His blood, but in
heaven they will be put back in the hymn book. I guess that may be the
reason the Lord isn't going to embarrass some of those folk by taking
them into heaven, because they would have to sing about the blood
there.

The change of the pronoun from "us" to "them" is important. They
are praising the Lamb for those yet to be saved on the earth—the tribulation saints.

"A kingdom and priests" refers to the tribulation saints. The
church will not reign on the earth, but over the earth.

MYRIADS OF ANGELS JOIN THE SONG

**And I beheld, and I heard the voice of many angels
round about the throne and the beasts and the elders:**

and the number of them was ten thousand times ten thousand, and thousands of thousands;

Saying with a loud voice, Worthy is the Lamb that was slain to receive power, and riches, and wisdom, and strength, and honour, and glory, and blessing [Rev. 5:11–12].

And I saw, and I heard a voice of many angels round about the throne and the living creatures and the elders, and the number of them was ten thousands of ten thousands (myriads), and thousands of thousands, saying with a great voice, Worthy is the Lamb that hath been slain to take the power, and riches, and wisdom, and might, and honor, and glory, and blessing.

When John says, "ten thousand times ten thousand, and thousands of thousands," I think that he means they were innumerable. In effect John says, "At first I looked and I saw a company of angels around the elders, and they were singing—and I thought that was great. But all of a sudden I looked out yonder and, boy, there was a crowd which I could not count!" Nobody could have counted them. A computer couldn't count them. God's created intelligences were praising Him. My friend, I do not know why you want to go to heaven if you do not want to worship and praise Him down here.

UNIVERSAL WORSHIP OF THE SAVIOR AND SOVEREIGN

And every creature which is in heaven, and on the earth, and under the earth, and such as are in the sea, and all that are in them, heard I saying, Blessing, and honour, and glory, and power, be unto him that sitteth upon the throne, and unto the Lamb for ever and ever.

And the four beasts said, Amen. And the four and twenty elders fell down and worshipped him that liveth for ever and ever [Rev. 5:13–14].

Every animate creature of God joins in this universal act of worship, both in heaven and earth. Evidently, the animals in the earth and the fish in the sea join in this volume of praise! The living creatures add their amen to it, and the church falls down in silent adoration and praise.

If I could, I would sing the "Hallelujah Chorus," for as we come to the end of this very remarkable scene in heaven, we see that all praise and honor and worship must go to the Lord Jesus Christ. If you are not in the habit of praising and worshiping Him, why don't you start right now?

BIBLIOGRAPHY
(Recommended for Further Study)

Barnhouse, Donald Grey. *Revelation, an Expository Commentary*. Grand Rapids, Michigan: Zondervan Publishing House, 1971.

Criswell, W. A. *Expository Sermons on Revelation*. Grand Rapids, Michigan: Zondervan Publishing House, 1966.

Epp, Theodore H. *Practical Studies in Revelation*. Lincoln, Nebraska: Back to the Bible Broadcast, 1969.

Gaebelein, Arno C. *The Revelation*. Neptune, New Jersey: Loizeaux Brothers, 1915.

Hoyt, Herman A. *The Revelation of the Lord Jesus Christ*. Winona Lake, Indiana: Brethren Missionary Herald, 1966.

Ironside, H. A. *Lectures on the Book of Revelation*. Neptune, New Jersey: Loizeaux Brothers, 1960. (Especially good for young converts.)

Larkin, Clarence. *The Book of Revelation*. Philadelphia, Pennsylvania: Published by the Author, 1919. (Includes fine charts.)

Lindsey, Hal. *There's a New World Coming*. Santa Ana, California: Vision House Publishers, 1973.

McGee, J. Vernon. *Reveling Through Revelation*. 2 vols. Pasadena, California: Thru the Bible Books, 1962.

Newell, William R. *The Book of Revelation*. Chicago, Illinois: Moody Press, 1935.

Phillips, John. *Exploring Revelation*. Chicago, Illinois: Moody Press, 1974.

Ryrie, Charles C. *Revelation*. Chicago, Illinois: Moody Press, 1968. (A fine, inexpensive survey.)

Scott, Walter. *Exposition of the Revelation of Jesus Christ.* London: Pickering and Inglis, n.d.

Seiss, J. A. *The Apocalypse, Lectures on the Book of Revelation.* Grand Rapids, Michigan: Zondervan Publishing House, 1957.

Smith, J. B. *A Revelation of Jesus Christ.* Scottsdale, Pennsylvania: Herald Press, 1961

Strauss, Lehman. *The Book of Revelation.* Neptune, New Jersey: Loizeaux Brothers, 1964.

Walvoord, John F. *The Revelation of Jesus Christ.* Chicago, Illinois: Moody Press, 1966 (Excellent comprehensive treatment.)